Praise for *Female Founders' Playbook*

'An incredible resource for the next generation of founders. Anne Boden lays out a practical playbook for starting and scaling high-growth businesses, with first-hand advice from some of the UK's top female entrepreneurs and investors.' BRENT HOBERMAN, EXECUTIVE CHAIRMAN AND FOUNDER, FOUNDERS FACTORY

'As a trailblazing female fintech entrepreneur, Anne Boden knows well the many barriers that the world throws up for women-owned businesses – and what it takes to achieve success in spite of these. This book is a fantastic testimony to the power and potential of women entrepreneurs and serves as an invaluable guide for women seeking to unlock these attributes within themselves.' CHERIE BLAIR CBE KC

'If you have an idea for a better way of doing things, this book will show you how to transform your vision and experience into a scalable business step by step. Based on her own experience and that of other women entrepreneurs who have succeeded in founding businesses that have made a mark, Anne Boden unveils the challenges – including those that are unique to women founders – on the road to leading a high-growth enterprise and then shows you how to navigate them successfully. A vital guide for any aspiring entrepreneur!' HERMINIA IBARRA, CHARLES HANDY PROFESSOR OF ORGANIZATIONAL BEHAVIOUR, LONDON BUSINESS SCHOOL

'You'll read this the first time for Anne Boden's engaging style and the wealth of experience she and her contributors share from their first-hand knowledge. You'll read it again, having been inspired to take the plunge and start a business, for the practical, comprehensive advice she provides. This is a real "how-to" manual that demystifies the intimidating aspects of founding and scaling a business. Roll on the "Female Founder Mafia"!' ANN FRANCKE OBE, CHIEF EXECUTIVE, CHARTERED MANAGEMENT INSTITUTE

T0049508

'Fuelled by the wisdom and fire of a founder who's blazed her own trail, *Female Founder's Playbook* doesn't sugar-coat the challenges. What it lays out, invaluably, are tested strategies to get over them. Whether you're just starting out or scaling your empire, this book is a must-have roadmap to entrepreneurial success.' LEO JOHNSON, HEAD OF DISRUPTION AND INNOVATION, PWC

Female Founders' Playbook

Insights from the superwomen who have made it

Anne Boden

KoganPage

First published in Great Britain and the United States in 2024 by Kogan Page Limited

2nd Floor, 45 Gee Street	8 W 38th Street, Suite 902	4737/23 Ansari Road
London	New York, NY 10018	Daryaganj
EC1V 3RS	USA	New Delhi 110002
United Kingdom		India
www.koganpage.com		

Kogan Page books are printed on paper from sustainable forests.

ISBNs
Hardback   978 1 3986 1637 0
Paperback 978 1 3986 1615 8
Ebook   978 1 3986 1636 3

British Library Cataloguing-in-Publication Data
A CIP record for this book is available from the British Library.

Library of Congress Cataloging-in-Publication Data
Names: Boden, Anne (Banking entrepreneur), author.
Title: Female founders' playbook : insights from the superwomen who have made it / Anne Boden.
Description: London, United Kingdom ; New York, NY : Kogan Page, 2024. | Includes bibliographical references and index.
Identifiers: LCCN 2023054576 (print) | LCCN 2023054577 (ebook) | ISBN 9781398616158 (paperback) | ISBN 9781398616370 (hardback) | ISBN 9781398616363 (ebook)
Subjects: LCSH: Women executives. | Leadership in women. | Creative ability in business. | Success in business.
Classification: LCC HD6054.3 .B64 2024 (print) | LCC HD6054.3 (ebook) | DDC 658.4/09082–dc23/eng/20231229
LC record available at https://lccn.loc.gov/2023054576
LC ebook record available at https://lccn.loc.gov/2023054577

Typeset by Hong Kong FIVE Workshop, Hong Kong
Print production managed by Jellyfish
Printed and bound by CPI Group (UK) Ltd, Croydon CR0 4YY

Contents

About the author

Anne Boden is the founder and former CEO of Starling Bank.
Anne began her 30-year career in the finance sector as a graduate trainee with Lloyds Bank, where she became one of the creators of CHAPS, the same-day payments system. Executive positions followed at Standard Chartered Bank and UBS before she moved on to head up global transaction banking across 34 countries for ABN Amro and RBS.

In 2012, Anne was headhunted to become Chief Operating Officer of Allied Irish Bank (AIB), with a brief to turn around the then debt-ridden bank which had been taken over by the Irish government. Although the bank was returned to profitability, the experience confirmed a view which had been growing in Anne's mind for some time: there was something very wrong with existing banking practices. While everyone else was desperately trying to reinstate the established business of finance that had been ripped apart by the global credit crunch and subsequent government bailouts, it was all underpinned by cumbersome legacy systems and inbuilt bureaucracy that had arguably contributed to the problem in the first place. Anne formed a vision for a new digital bank that would use the latest technology to put the customer first and give them ever-greater choice.

Despite initial scepticism from her peers and potential investors, the mobile bank Anne created in 2014 has gone on to become one of modern banking's biggest success stories, winning multiple awards, and is now approaching 3.8 million new customers.

After starting life as the UK's first mobile-only current account, Starling now offers business accounts, joint accounts and a marketplace offering a range of partnerships with complementary financial partners.

Anne, who has been named by Forbes as one of the top 50 women working in tech worldwide, stepped aside as CEO of Starling Bank in May 2023. She is a regular speaker and commentator on the role of fintech in modern life, both in the UK and on the international circuit. She is also a published author of *Banking On It: How I disrupted an industry and changed the way we manage our money forever* (Penguin Business, 2021) and *The Money Revolution: Easy ways to manage your finances in a digital world* (Kogan Page, 2019).

Anne Boden was awarded an MBE in the 2018 Queen's Birthday Honours, for services to fintech.

Contributors

SOPHIE ADELMAN

Sophie Adelman is a serial entrepreneur, angel investor and passionate believer in the power of learning to unlock lives. Sophie co-founded and served on the board of Multiverse, a leading future of work scale-up building an outstanding alternative to university through apprenticeships. Her most recent start-up, One Garden, which focuses on lifelong learning, was sold to Saga Plc in 2023. She was previously Entrepreneur in Residence at Index Ventures and European Head of Sales/GM for Hired. Sophie currently lives in Germany with her husband and two young children and is a Board Member of Elizabeth's Smile Foundation and the Munich International School. She has an MBA from Stanford Graduate School of Business and a MA (Cantab) from Cambridge University.

JUNE ANGELIDES*

Born in London and raised in Lagos, June Angelides joined Samos Investments in 2018, investing in high-growth European businesses. She is a generalist investor and has led Samos' investments into Jude, Ruka Hair and Mantle. She has a small but growing portfolio of angel investments into female-founded businesses including Bloom Money, Odin, By Rotation, Sojo and Amela. She also runs a Micro fund on Odin, Levare Ventures, to invest into early-stage African start-ups.

Prior to being an investor, June started the first child-friendly coding school in the UK, Mums in Tech, which taught over 250 women to code in three years. She also held roles on the Venture Debt Team and Early Stage Banking Team at Silicon Valley Bank. An active part of the tech and start-up ecosystem, she sits on the boards of Jude, Flair, Ruka and Everpress, is a mentor at Oxford University and runs mentoring circles for founders and aspiring VCs. She is passionate about flexible working and getting more women and girls into tech. She is a columnist at the *Financial Times*. She has been named by the *Financial Times* as the sixth most influential tech leader and by *Computer Weekly* as one of the most influential women in tech.

June received an Honorary Fellowship at the Institute of Engineering and Technology and has been awarded an MBE for services to women in technology.

TANIA BOLER

Tania Boler is the founder and President of Elvie. Until 2022, she was founder and CEO, during which time, she built the business to around $100 million revenue and market leader for premium breast pumps in the UK and USA.

Founded in 2013, Elvie brings together a team of world-class engineers, designers and business minds to develop extraordinary technology and products that improve women's lives, revolutionizing categories which had been overlooked for many years, including breast pumps and pelvic floor health. Elvie now has six products across two categories and has received international awards and recognition for its products, including being named *TIME* Magazine 100 Greatest Inventions and winning prestigious Red Dot design awards.

Before founding Elvie in 2013, Tania was the Global Director of Research and Innovation at Marie Stopes International, focusing on sexual health in developing countries. She has a PhD in HIV and teenage pregnancy in South Africa and has published widely on women's health and rights. In addition, Tania worked extensively in South Asia and Africa promoting research into maternal and reproductive health – with a focus on HIV and teenage pregnancy – and worked with the UN to launch the first-ever curriculum on sexuality education. In 2021, Tania was named *Glamour*'s Women of the Year: Technology Gamechanger.

JENNY CAMPBELL

Jenny is an ex-career banker turned business-turnaround specialist and cash machine entrepreneur.

After leaving school at 16 to begin her working life counting cash in a bank branch, she climbed through the ranks to become one of the few senior female bankers at the time in the UK. Following 30 years in the banking trade, Jenny left the corporate world in 2006 in pursuit of a new challenge – to turn around a failing cash machine business owned by RBS. Jenny launched a major operational restructure of Hanco ATM Systems, turning it from a business that was making a huge loss in competitive markets to a thriving, profitable entity operating across Europe.

In the midst of the turnaround process and at the height of the financial crash, Jenny was tasked with selling the business. However, she saw that the business had real potential and wasn't ready to give up on it or the people in it. So she decided to buy out the business from RBS and become the majority shareholder, later relaunching it as YourCash Europe Ltd.

The cash machine company quickly expanded to become a leading provider of ATMs to the retail market across Europe, handling millions of ATM transactions and processing billions in cash value. Ten years on from taking the business under her wing, Jenny sold YourCash in October 2016 for £50 million.

Previously awarded Business Woman of the Year, Jenny brings feisty northern grit to the fifteenth series of the hit BBC TV show *Dragons' Den*, sticking true to her favourite business motto: 'Live by corporate standards, but breathe like an entrepreneur.'

ALEX DEPLEDGE

Alex Depledge is a serial British entrepreneur, and currently CEO of Resi and Independent Director of Persimmon Homes.

Resi is the UK's largest residential home extension company and a leading tech scaleup business. Created to modernize the architectural sector, Resi has helped over 6,000 homeowners to transform their homes, providing everything from design and contractor introductions to home finance options.

Before Resi, in 2012 Alex set up Hassle, Europe's largest domestic cleaning marketplace, in partnership with Julianne Coleman with whom she later founded Resi. The business experienced hyper-growth from the start and raised $6 million from venture firm Accel Partners (the first backers of Facebook and Spotify) to scale across Europe. Alex brokered two mergers and acquisitions (M&A) deals, with the latter resulting in the acquisition of Hassle for €32 million by a German company.

Alex was a Non-Executive Director of Edited (2016–20), a fashion analytics software used by leading retailers in the USA and Europe, including Inditex and Arcadia. Between 2017 and 2021 Alex sat on the board of London LEAP, chaired by the Mayor of London, which is responsible for over £100 million of investment into London's culture and communities. She was also part of the launch of Founders Pledge, where 50 UK tech entrepreneurs pledge 2 per cent of their exit proceeds to charity.

Alex was educated at the University of Nottingham and the University of Chicago, and began her career as a consultant for Accenture. In 2016 she was made an MBE for services to the sharing economy. She is a regular TV, podcast and radio commentator and an outspoken advocate of the importance of wellbeing in the home.

CHRISTY FOSTER

Christy Foster is the MD of Online4baby, a family business she founded with her younger sister Cheryl.

Brought up by a single mother who had three jobs to try to make ends meet, Christy's route to entrepreneurial success began at the age of 12, when she worked on a market stall before and after school each day to earn enough money for a decent lunch. In her teens she embarked on several money-making ventures, including selling jewellery and gift boxes at factories, mills and hairdressing salons, earning enough in the run-up to one Christmas to buy her mum a car.

Realizing her strength was buying and selling, Christy, who is highly dyslexic, slightly autistic and has just three GCSEs to her name, later began buying bric-a-brac, furniture and antiques and selling them on markets around Greater Manchester, working seven days a week for up to 16 hours a day. Nursery items proved great sellers and Christy decided to concentrate on these as well as maternity wear. As her business grew, her husband Darren and sister Cheryl joined her and they branched out to markets in Yorkshire and into wholesaling, buying seconds from big brands and catalogue retailers. When eBay took off, Christy switched her focus to this platform and her business became the largest eBay baby store in Europe. She became one of the first eBay millionaires, but realized she could have her own website, and Online4baby was born in 2011. Under Christy's leadership, the pure-play e-commerce business has grown exponentially.

JOANNA JENSEN

Former Investment Banker Joanna Jensen is the founder of the UK's number one baby and child personal care brand, Childs Farm, having created the brand in 2010 as a result of her own daughters' sensitive and eczema prone skin.

Supplying fun, fragrant, natural and sustainable washing and bathing products for sensitive skin, the brand first launched into mainstream retailers in 2014 and within five years from launch become the number one brand in the baby and child toiletries category.

In 2022 Joanna sold the majority of Childs Farm for £36.75 million to PZ Cussons Plc, the branded consumer goods business and owner of well-known brands such as St.Tropez, Imperial Leather and Carex.

Joanna is an active supporter of entrepreneurs, in particular female-founded businesses. She is a mentor to the next generation of entrepreneurs through Imperial College's Venture Mentoring service, and sits on the Advisory Board of Buy Women Built, which drives awareness of female-founded business to UK consumers and investors.

Passionate about sustainability, Joanna is a Sustainability Advisor to the British Beauty Council.

With a lifelong passion for horses, Joanna supports the charity Riding for the Disabled, and from this became a part-owner of Paralympic dressage horse, Keystone Dawn Chorus. She is an active supporter of the British Paralympics Association, and is Chair of their Philanthropic Group, the Parallel Club.

ZANDRA MOORE*

Zandra Moore is the co-founder and CEO of Panintelligence and is a tech entrepreneur specialising in data. Zandra is passionate about enabling more women in the tech industry, improving gender equality and increasing investment in female-founded businesses. Earlier roles in tech instilled a desire to make a change in the mostly male-led sector.

Panintelligence, has grown to be a globally recognized embedded analytics provider for software as a service vendors. Its rapid and secure platform, pi, gives customers self-service dashboards, interactive reports and predictive analytics using causal AI. This allows users to unlock the value of data and put data visualization into the heart of workflows.

Zandra's unwavering energy led to the creation of LeanIn Leeds, No Code Lab and the Yorkshire Growth Tech Group, all with the focus of supporting and championing diversity in tech. With this experience, Zandra also become a member of the UK Government's women-led high-growth enterprise taskforce.

Recently, to expand her interest in supporting other entrepreneurs, Zandra became an angel investor and active mentor into female founders through Ada Ventures and various female founder incubators such as Bruntwood SciTech.

Zandra's commitment and dedication to the UK technology sector has led to numerous awards and industry recognition, most recently the Emerging Entrepreneur Award at the Enterprise Awards 2023, Outstanding Entrepreneur Award from Northern Power Women 2023 and her Panintelligence Software winning BI Solution of the Year at the British Data Awards 2023.

DEEPALI NANGIA*

Deepali is a Partner at Speedinvest, a pan-European VC fund with a focus on finding, funding and supporting investment in female and diverse founders.

Deepali also co-founded Alma Angels, a community set up to increase the number of female angel investors in Europe who fund female-founded companies. She has angel invested in and mentored multiple female-founded companies, including PensionBee, Fluus, Kama Labs, Sano Genetics, Shell Works, SideQuest, Juno Bio, Flown, Okko Health, Vine Health, Vaayu and Yhangry, among others.

In 2021 Deepali won UKBAA's Angel Investor of the Year award.

Originally from Kolkata, India, with a background in investment banking, private equity and operations, Deepali has a keen interest in technologies that are solving society's large problems in sectors such as digital health, femtech, climate and education tech.

ROMI SAVOVA

Romi Savova founded PensionBee in 2014 to simplify pension savings in the UK, following a difficult pension transfer experience of her own. As the Chief Executive Officer, she has played a pivotal role in advancing consumer standards in the pensions industry, from reducing transfer times to campaigning for the full abolition of exit fees.

Operating in the £1 trillion market of defined contribution pension assets, PensionBee has grown rapidly through its direct-to-consumer marketing activities, creating a household brand name for the mass market. The company had over £3.4 billion in assets under administration and 198,000 invested customers as at 31 March 2023. PensionBee has consistently maintained a customer retention rate in excess of 95 per cent and an 'excellent' Trustpilot rating, reflecting its commitment to outstanding customer service. PensionBee is admitted to trading on the Premium Segment of the London Stock Exchange Main Market (LON:PBEE).

Romi is also a member of the government's Pensions Dashboards Programme Steering Group, which was set up to advise on the delivery of pensions dashboards.

Prior to founding PensionBee, Romi worked at Goldman Sachs, Morgan Stanley and Credit Benchmark, holding varied roles in risk management, investment banking and financial technology. Romi received an MBA from Harvard Business School as a George F. Baker scholar and graduated summa cum laude from Emory University.

DAME STEPHANIE SHIRLEY

Dame Stephanie Shirley CH, also known as Steve, is a workplace revolutionary and successful IT entrepreneur turned ardent venture philanthropist. At 89 years old, her story has many strands which, woven together, have produced a lifetime of exceptional achievements.

Dame Stephanie arrived in Britain in 1939, as an unaccompanied five-year-old Kindertransport refugee. This defining experience equipped her with fortitude at a very young age and made her determined to live a life worth saving.

In 1962, she started a software house, Freelance Programmers, and pioneered radical new flexible work practices that changed the landscape for women working in technology. She went on to create a global business and a personal fortune which she shared with her colleagues, making millionaires of 70 of her staff at no cost to anyone but herself.

Since retiring in 1993, Dame Stephanie's life has been dedicated to venture philanthropy in the fields of IT and autism. She initially founded Autism at Kingwood in 1994 to support her late son Giles, and her charitable Shirley Foundation went on to make grants of nearly £70 million. It spent out in 2018 in favour of Autistica, the UK's national autism research charity founded by Dame Stephanie. In 2009/10 she served as the UK's first ever national Ambassador for Philanthropy.

Dame Stephanie's memoir *Let It Go* was first published in 2012 and re-published in 2019 for worldwide distribution. During lockdown in 2020, Dame Stephanie produced her second book, *So To Speak*, a collection of 29 of her speeches given over the last 40 years. All proceeds from the book go to Autistica.

SAM SMITH*

Entrepreneur Sam Smith is the founder, former CEO and adviser to finnCap Group Plc.

Sam established finnCap in 2007, having orchestrated the management buyout of a small broking division of J M Finn & Co Limited, a private client stockbroking firm. By 2010, directors and employees had purchased the remaining 50.1 per cent of the equity retained by J M Finn. In 2018, finnCap acquired Cavendish Corporate Finance, a leading UK M&A adviser, floated on AIM in 2018, and began trading as finnCap Group Plc. Sam was the first female chief executive of a City stockbroking firm and has worked on over 200 transactions, initial public offerings (IPO) and secondary fund raisings. Under her leadership, finnCap became a leading advisory firm for the business of tomorrow. The sector specialist service offering ranged from equity capital markets and IPO, to plc strategic advisory, debt advisory, M&A and private growth capital, as well as net-zero and sustainability consultancy services through investment in Energise. finnCap Group includes finnCap Capital Markets and finnCap Cavendish to form a market-leading strategic M&A firm that has a global reach through its membership of Oaklins.

Sam is now an adviser to scale-up businesses and a non-executive director on the board of Sumer Group Ltd. She is an adviser to the ScaleUp Institute, the not-for-profit whose mission is to make the UK the best place in the world to start and grow a business, as well as a private equity backed professional services business aiming to be the UK champion of small and medium-sized enterprises. Sam is also passionate about empowering young people and helping them develop essential life skills. She is spearheading a campaign for entrepreneurship to be integrated into the school curriculum, and works with organizations such as YourGamePlan, icanyoucantoo and Modern Muse to help create a fairer foundation for young people, irrespective of their background.

Sam qualified as a Chartered Accountant at KPMG. Her awards include 2010 Business XL, 2009 Business XL, Power Top 50 – number three in the City, National Business Woman of the Future Award and the Top 100 Financial Rising Stars Award.

HELEN STEERS*

Helen is a Partner in Pantheon's European Investment Team and Pantheon's senior manager for listed global private equity investment trust, Pantheon International Plc. She is a member of the International Investment Committee, European Investment Committee and Co-Investment Committee. Helen joined Pantheon in 2004 from Russell Investments in Paris where she was Managing Director with overall responsibility for private equity in Europe. Prior to joining Russell in 1999, Helen worked as Director, European Private Equity with the Caisse de dépôt et placement du Québec and was a senior investment manager at the Business Development Bank of Canada in Montréal. Helen received a BA and MA in Engineering from the University of Cambridge and an MBA from the University of Western Ontario in Canada. Helen is a past Chair and Council member of the British Private Equity and Venture Capital Association (BVCA) and served on the board and LP Council of Invest Europe. She is also a co-founder of Level 20, a non-profit organization established to inspire women to join and succeed in the private equity industry. Helen is bilingual in English and French, and proficient in German. She enjoys travelling, skiing and road cycling, and is an avid reader and classic film enthusiast.

CHECK WARNER*

Check Warner is one of the founding Partners of Ada Ventures, a seed venture capital fund with over £100 million under management, investing in breakthrough ideas for the hardest problems we face. Ada Ventures is backed by a group of mission aligned investors, including founders of Europe's biggest technology companies such as Wise and Supercell. Ada has invested in companies like Huboo, which is transforming fulfilment, Bubble, the UK's leading childcare marketplace, and Spill, which is opening access to mental health support. Ada Ventures is named after Ada Lovelace, the pioneering computer programmer and mathematician, who was never recognized during the time she lived for what she contributed to the advancement of technology and science. Check is also the co-founder of Diversity VC, a non-profit made up of interested individuals working in venture capital, who seek to increase diversity of thought in the venture and tech industry. In 2022 Check was awarded an MBE in the King's New Year's Honours List for services to diversity and inclusion in venture capital.

* Members of the women-led high-growth enterprise taskforce

Acknowledgements

The purpose of this book is to share the knowledge that I gained over my 10-year journey with Starling Bank – knowledge I wish I'd had when I started out. If you believe what you read here has helped you with your own start-up journey, then this book has done its job.

I didn't gain these insights in isolation, though. There have been hundreds, probably thousands, of people who have somehow contributed to what I now know and have shared here. Some by showing how it can be done better, others by demonstrating exactly how not to do it. My thanks go to you all.

There are also many individuals whom I would like to thank personally. I am hugely grateful for the help and support of Teena Lyons, a great friend and collaborator on my many initiatives over the last 15 years; Alexandra Frean, Starling Bank's Chief Corporate Affairs Officer, and Kam Hudson, my Executive Assistant. You all helped make this happen on an incredibly tight timescale. I am also grateful to the team at Kogan Page, and in particular Chris Cudmore, for keeping it on track.

A huge vote of thanks must also go to my fellow taskforce members, who gave up so much of their time, when they had so many other things to attend to elsewhere. These are: Angela Scott, founder of TC BioPharm; Deepali Nangia, a Partner at Speedinvest; Francesca (Check) Warner, a Partner at Ada Ventures; Helen Steers, a Partner at Pantheon Ventures; Jan Putnis, a Partner and Head of financial regulation group Slaughter and May; Judith Hartley, CEO, British Business Investments; June Angelides, investor at Samos Investments; Sam Smith, founder of finnCap Group; and Zandra Moore, co-founder Panintelligence. Thanks also go to Sophie White of Strategy & PWC, who has been so helpful with the work of the taskforce.

As well as giving up even more of their time to be interviewed for the book, members of the taskforce also helped with introductions to other female entrepreneurs. This led to some illuminating interviews with Jenny Campbell, YourCash; Sophie Adelman, One Garden and Multiverse; Romi Savova, PensionBee; Tania Boler, Elvie; and Joanna Jensen, Childs Farm. I am very grateful to them all for sharing what they have learned – it was fascinating hearing their stories.

In addition, I would like to acknowledge the help and assistance of the Cabinet Office's Equality Unit, which has been a valuable resource. In particular, I'd like to thank Sue Beaumont-Staite, the Senior Policy Adviser, Gender Equality Division, and Paul Williamson, Head of Gender and Cross Equality Analysis, both at Equality Hub; and, at the Government Equalities Office, Gender Equality Division, both Barbara Collins, the Deputy Head, and Kevin Mantle, the Senior Policy Manager.

Finally, my grateful thanks go to all the people upon whom I have practised the art of CEO founder for the last few years, including Susanna Yallop, Chief People Officer at Starling Bank. Together, we all successfully transitioned Starling Bank from a start-up to one of the UK's greatest high-growth business success stories.

Introduction

The best entrepreneurs are female. Do you know why? They've had to fight so hard to succeed, *nothing* is going to stop them. We've all seen the statistics. It is common knowledge that female-led businesses raise less money, get less grant funding and always need to meet higher thresholds of standards. And, when they do raise funding, they need to sign away a larger share of their companies. Yet, when they get a break, female-led businesses produce astonishing returns for their investors. That is why I say that they make the very best entrepreneurs.

When I was asked to lead a government-backed taskforce to support female start-ups, I jumped at the chance. Specifically, I was attracted by its goal of encouraging female entrepreneurs to found and build high-growth businesses. Since entering the world of entrepreneurship in 2014 with the idea of Starling Bank, I have become depressingly familiar with the challenges that face female entrepreneurs who try to scale their businesses. Whether it is difficulty raising funding, or disproportionate and often-unfair press scrutiny, we face a constant uphill battle. Yet, if we could change this situation and female entrepreneurs were able to start companies at the same rate as their male counterparts, we could add £250 billion onto the UK's gross domestic product.[1]

Before we go into all the reasons why women should consider becoming entrepreneurs and share ideas on how we can help them succeed, let's start by defining 'high-growth business'. There's a bit of variation around the definition, but essentially the term refers to a start-up that experiences *exponential* growth. (I should also add that 'exponential' growth is mathematically impossible. While high-growth businesses grow rapidly, they can't grow at this rate forever because they would eventually own an entire market.) Both the Organisation for Economic Co-operation and Development (OECD) and Beauhurst define high-growth enterprises as those with average annualized growth greater than 20 per cent per annum over a three-year period.[2] Beauhurst also notes a number of other high-growth triggers such as equity investment, attending an accelerator or receiving a major grant. The venture capital (VC) world, on the other hand, seems to define it as 20 per cent growth month-on-month. Either way; we are referring to businesses that scale-up quickly and make their mark. There are around 46,000 high-growth businesses in the UK, each with the potential to disrupt their respective sectors by scaling at a rate significantly higher than all their competitors.[3] The ones that scale the most reach the coveted status of 'unicorn', which signifies a start-up with a valuation of over $1 billion.

The UK is a great country for starting up businesses and there is a strong eco system to support them, but most businesses, particularly female-led ones, seem to get to a certain point and then stop. They continue operations, but growth stagnates. There can be many reasons for this. They may not want to scale, or can't scale, or don't have the funding to do so. It's just too difficult to make the leap to the next stage. But, if we want to see more fast-growth businesses like Starling Bank, with all the advantages they bring with them to employment levels and our economy, then we need to help them get over the difficult bit.

From a UK PLC point of view, this matters. A lot. High-growth enterprises and tech unicorns are the organizations that will fuel our future, unlocking growth and productivity in the UK. Once businesses reach a certain size, they are always transformative for their national economies, not to mention having a substantial impact on the global economy too. It is therefore in the UK's best interest to support the development of as many home-grown high-growth businesses as possible. Right now, though, half the population of the UK is largely excluded from taking part in this endeavour. Women entrepreneurs routinely receive less than a 2 per cent share of the UK's multi-billion pound VC funding each year, funding that is crucial to help them scale their start-ups.[4]

Think of how much better off we'd be if we were able to release the enthusiasm and ideas of 50 per cent of the population. Doing so would vastly increase the chances of the UK producing the next Google, or Amazon, or, dare I say it, Starling Bank. It just seems incredible that in this day and age we're still not making use of half of our resources. The UK is tackling this challenge with one hand tied behind its back.

There have been moves to level the playing field. The taskforce is clear evidence of this and there has also been a marked growth in more inclusive venture funds. This has, in great part, been encouraged by the work of a number of organizations, including Diversity VC and Level 20, which have made great inroads in educating the VC community, helping them to set standards for the future and adjust policies to become more diverse and inclusive. (Details of organizations of note are included in 'Further information', page 189). Indeed, many of the senior women who head funds that prioritize support for female founders participated in the taskforce and have contributed to this book. These funds are taking a new approach to fund and support entrepreneurs from all sorts of different backgrounds. They are performing really well, too.

It is, however, early days. Despite all the hard work that is going on, these changes will take a while to have a significant impact. In the meantime, the onus is very much on female founders to pick their way around this complicated and often secretive industry. But, where do they start?

My own background was very corporate, having spent more than 30 years working for major banks before deciding to start a business. When I began my entrepreneurial journey, I didn't have any contacts in this strange new world and had to make a conscious effort to learn everything I could. I listened to every single podcast coming out of Silicon Valley, read every blog, devoured countless books, watched every video and went to all the big events to network like crazy. It was complete immersion in the start-up scene. I didn't always feel comfortable going to the events, not least because I was very conscious that I didn't look like anyone else there. I was a woman in her early 50s, whereas nearly everyone else was male and in their 20s and 30s. To say they were sceptical about what I had to offer would be an understatement.

Ten years on, the entrepreneurial environment is a little bit better, thanks to the tireless campaigning of a number of inspirational women who are trying to make things fairer. Even so, the start-up scene can still be a bit of a minefield for women. This is the reason I decided to produce this playbook to help the next generation of female entrepreneurs in the hope that many, many more will consider building high-growth ventures. The book runs alongside the taskforce report, which gives a snapshot of where we are now, along with recommendations of the high-level changes needed to help more female-led enterprises to succeed. The goal of *Female Founder's Playbook* is to create a practical, interesting resource showing prospective female entrepreneurs how to get started with their own ventures. We explore everything from how best to position a business, to building a winning start-up team, to getting access to finance and growth capital, to leading these ground-breaking enterprises. A lot of time can be wasted by going to the wrong resources; we're aiming to help female-led start-ups by providing all the information they need in one place – this playbook.

To provide the most up-to-date information, I invited my fellow task-force members to collaborate on the book, along with some of the UK's leading female entrepreneurs. It has been fascinating to hear about their lived experiences, and we've got viewpoints from both the VC and start-up side. Many of the challenges I've heard about resonate with my own, and I greatly enjoyed hearing about how my fellow female entrepreneurs over-came them. We can learn a lot from the stories of those that have succeeded.

It is important to state from the very outset that this book is not about 'fixing' women. I've read and listened to far too many 'thought pieces' tell-ing women how to get over imposter syndrome, or how to speak up for themselves, or behave in a more credible way to make themselves acceptable in a male-orientated system. Each time I come across one, it makes me want to shout: why do we need to fix women? As I said from the outset: women make exceptional entrepreneurs. And, as I show in Chapter 1, we also have a unique range of skills that actually make us particularly suited to start-up life. We're not interested in 'fixing' the system, either, to push it far over in the other direction. Inevitably, one subject that always comes up in any discussion about levelling the playing field is quotas. Should we be advocat-ing hard to force more investors to invest in women? Interestingly, the party that has pushed back the most on this concept is female entrepreneurs. Female founders want to receive investment on their own merits, based on the strength of their idea, rather than because they fit into a certain demo-graphic bucket. No, women don't need fixing, and we don't want the system fixed so it is unfair to any other group either. Nevertheless, until we move into a time when female entrepreneurs are treated *on a par* with their male counterparts, they need to know how to navigate the system to make the most of the incredible talents and skills they have. Again, this is something this book hopes to address. *Female Founder's Playbook* is intended to be a companion for female entrepreneurs setting out on the journey. Hopefully, it will be an inspiration for those that believe something needs to be done and that they are the person to do it.

The obvious retort from any would-be female entrepreneur is: if it is this hard, why would I bother? I have a certain amount of sympathy with that objection. It is not easy being a trailblazer. However, I would argue that the reasons to go ahead absolutely outweigh those against.

The first thing to make clear is: it will be difficult to create a high-growth business, but not quite as difficult as the headline data might appear to indicate. The stats do deserve greater scrutiny. While a lot is made from the fact that just 2 per cent of funds go to female founders, this only represents *female-only* teams. In cases where there is a female founder working along-side male co-founders, these businesses account for about 20 per cent of VC money. The latest research by the Rose Review suggests that about 20 per cent of all businesses are now run by women, up from 16 per cent in 2018.[5] The numbers are still not ideal, but they do show that female entrepreneurs are breaking through in greater numbers than some figures suggest.

Something else that deserves more scrutiny is the number of pitches made. It's not a straight 50:50 gender split. Just 25 per cent of pitch decks are presented by female-founded businesses, or those with a female as part of the broader team.[6] This seems to indicate the problem does not solely lie in funding. It shows that not enough female-led teams are going for funding. The reasons why are not clear. We don't know if women are less interested in beginning high-growth businesses, or have self-selected out because they don't think they will be able to get investment. Among some women at least, there is most likely an underlying school of thought that, with odds like this, why would anyone want to become an entrepreneur? We could, and should, so easily change this, particularly when there are so many examples of successful female entrepreneurs who make inspiring role models.

In Europe over the past 15 years, at least 87 female co-founders have led their businesses to a successful exit, including 15 female-led initial public offerings (IPOs). The UK leads the European pack in scaling and then exit-ing businesses, accounting for 31 of those exits, with four of the top 10 by exit value also from the UK.[7] Included in this number were Andrea Spezzi, who founded Orchard Therapeutics in 2015 and floated it with a $1.3 billion valuation in 2018, Compass Pathways' Ekaterina Malievskaia who saw her firm to a $544 million IPO in 2021, and Romi Savova, the founder of PensionBee, who is one of the contributors to this book. PensionBee also floated in 2021, in this case with a $550 million valuation. The final top 10 female founder from the UK is Sarah Gilbert, the founder of Vaccitech, based in Oxford, which was valued at $464 million at its IPO.

The UK has also produced a veritable herd of female-led unicorns, too. My own business Starling Bank reached that status in 2021. There's also Darktrace, co-founded by Poppy Gustaffson, PatSnap led by Guan Dian, Lendable with Victoria Van Lennep, and FNZ Group with Kate Hyndman, to name but a few.[8] The goal is to see many, many more female-led unicorns, but this will only be possible if more women take the plunge and start businesses with the potential to scale.

Another aim of this book, and perhaps one of the most important, is to encourage women to think differently about entrepreneurialism. Founding, then scaling, a high-growth business is a great career choice for so many women. Those who have done it say it is the best, most fulfilling move they have ever made.

There are a lot of reasons why women choose to go it alone and launch a start-up. Some are motivated by a burning desire to prove themselves, or to bring something worthwhile to the market. As a founder, everything starts and finishes with you. Others enjoy the intellectual challenge of plotting a path towards success and overcoming the barriers along the way. For many, it is the only way to properly use their skills and develop their career. Each of these reasons contributed to giving me the impetus to found Starling Bank and then battle through the various challenges.

While it can be tough (and, at times, running a high-growth business will be the toughest thing anyone has done in their whole life), it will also be the most exciting and exhilarating choice you'll ever make. The buzz derived from the impact you can make is huge. Yes, it is a rollercoaster, with fantastic wins at the top and devastating losses at the bottom, but the satisfaction derived from the wins far, far outweighs the bad times.

Becoming an entrepreneur is about so much more than what you want from a career. It is about what you want from your life. The two will be inexorably intertwined, because you will need to commit to giving it your all. But if it works out it will transform everything.

It will get easier. When there are enough female founder success stories, it will become self-generating. You may have heard of the so-called PayPal mafia. This is the all-male founding team of PayPal, who used their earnings to go on and found many other successful ventures such as Tesla, SpaceX, LinkedIn and Palantir. In fact, Silicon Valley is filled with enterprises launched with the money and expertise of the founders of the payment technology giant. Successful founders almost invariably go on to run, or at least invest in, multiple further enterprises (not least because it is a lot easier second time around, once the founder has a proven reputation and money behind them). Now think of the progress we will make when many of the female founders featured in the lists above start investing in the next generation. We could have our own female founder mafia. Or perhaps I am getting ahead of myself. Right now, though, female founders can take advantage of the wisdom of those that have gone before them that features in this book. The value of our combined first-hand knowledge cannot be underestimated. Then, it is up to individuals to use the talents they have, navigate the system as best they can and prove to the world that they do indeed make the best entrepreneurs. We *know* you are going to make an impression.

Notes

[1] A Rose. The Alison Rose review of female entrepreneurship, 2019. assets.publishing.service. gov.uk/government/uploads/system/uploads/attachment_data/file/784324/RoseReview_Digital_FINAL.PDF (archived at https://perma.cc/Z5GL-4LWS)

[2] Beahurst. High-growth business: What constitutes high-growth? Beahurst, 22 November 2018. www.beauhurst.com/blog/high-growth-business (archived at https://perma.cc/RQQ2-XFEQ)

[3] Beahurst. Top 200 women-powered businesses, Beauhurst and JP Morgan, 2023. assets. jpmprivatebank.com/content/dam/jpm-wm-aem/other/top-200-uk/Top200_Women-Powered_Businesses_2023.pdf (archived at https://perma.cc/7XKE-3HLF)

[4] A Wood. Only 2% of VC funding goes to female and ethnic minority founded businesses, Startup Magazine, nd. startupsmagazine.co.uk/article-only-2-vc-funding-goes-female-and-ethnic-minority-founded-businesses (archived at https://perma.cc/HT2B-UQ4K); T Bradshaw, D Thomas and M Murgia, The UK's female entrepreneurs battling for a fair share of funding, *Financial Times*, 30 September 2021. www.ft.com/content/a4336c48-0976-42a3-9a75-58ab334c41f3 (archived at https://perma.cc/VWP8-7BT9)

[5] Nat West. The Rose Review 2023 outlines new initiatives to help more women to start and build thriving businesses, Nat West, 22 February 2023. www.natwest.com/business/insights/business-management/leadership-and-development/rose-review-2023-new-initiatives-to-build-thriving-businesses.html (archived at https://perma.cc/8FNQ-GU4T)

[6] D Taylor. Combating the stats: The 200 Billion Club launches to support female entrepreneurs, Tech EU, 8 February 2022. tech.eu/2022/02/08/combating-the-stats-the-200-billion-club-launches-to-support-female-entrepreneurs (archived at https://perma.cc/H3K9-YFC4)

[7] I Woodford and F Scolari. Female entrepreneurs banked a record number of exits in Europe last year, Sifted, 26 January 2022. sifted.eu/articles/female-europe-record-exits-2021 (archived at https://perma.cc/CW8Y-PATZ)

[8] S de Bruin and M Munoz. European women in VC, IDC, May 2022. europeanwomeninvc. idcinteractive.net/104 (archived at https://perma.cc/4HQG-ERAS)

CHAPTER ONE

Calling all reluctant entrepreneurs

There are few life experiences as exhilarating as starting out with an idea and turning it into a globally recognized business, employing hundreds, even thousands, of people and turning over tens of millions, even billions.

The odds are stacked against creating a successful high-growth business, whether you are a male or female founder. There can only be a certain number of global giants, however innovative and disruptive a new contender might seem, not least because there are finite markets for any product or service. Then, there is a dizzying range of reasons why certain entrepreneurial ventures never take off, even when everything seems to point to potentially stratospheric growth. Even the best business ideas can fail if the market shifts, or if there is political upheaval, or new regulations are passed. Alternatively, a competitor may enter the market with a product that is just that little better, or maybe not even that. It simply captures the zeitgeist. One of the most common reasons why entrepreneurial ambitions don't play out is a lack of capital.

For female founders, though, each of the above apply, plus there are *even more* barriers standing in the way of success, meaning businesses that are founded, led, owned or managed by women make up just over *a quarter* of the high-growth ecosystem of the UK. That is 13,255 ventures out of a total of 46,300.[1]

The quick and simplistic explanation as to why the chances of success are reduced for female entrepreneurs is access to funding. And, indeed, the statistics do bear this up. Less than a fifth of the money raised by start-ups goes to a founding team that includes a woman, and the average amount raised by women-only start-up teams is around four times lower than the equivalent raised by men-only teams.[2] There are multiple reasons why funding options might be less available to women, and we will explore many of them here, as well as putting forward some ideas on beating the odds. To begin with, though, we should look at another aspect to why we see fewer female entrepreneurs succeeding. Quite simply, there are fewer of them to begin with.

In the UK, just 11 per cent of start-ups are led by women-only teams.[3] Company incorporations with at least one female director represent around 34 per cent of total incorporations. This is a small increase over the past decade but nothing to shout about.[4] What appears to be happening is women are turning their backs on entrepreneurship as a career option. Their chances of creating a high-growth business are over before they have even begun.

There are many reasons why we need to redress the imbalance in opportunities for male and female entrepreneurs. Reasons over and above sheer fair play. We know that female-founded businesses deliver higher revenue – more than twice as much per dollar invested – than those founded by men.[5] In addition, women-owned firms create more jobs than their male-owned peers, and have a larger appetite for growth and success.[6] Yet, in order to realize these opportunities, we need to see more women stepping up.

Are you an entrepreneur?

I was a finalist in an Entrepreneur of the Year competition and being interviewed by the judges. It was a bit of a strange set up, me in a Mastermind-style chair at the end of a long table with 15 judges sat around it. One of the judges asked a question which took me aback. He said, 'Jenny, you are clearly a successful entrepreneur now – what took you so long?'

I was about 46 years old at the time, so it felt quite biting. I told him I had a strong work ethic within me. Going back 100 years, my grandparents were entrepreneurs, which is just the fancy word for running your own business. One of them ran a printing press and the other built houses. That spirit flowed through the generations. When I was 10 years old, I sewed soft toys and sold them to my mum's students at the college where she worked. By age 13, I was working in a newsagent, serving customers, selling products, and cashing up at the end of the day and then I groomed dogs every Saturday, charging £10. I spent 30 years climbing the corporate ladder with Nat West and RBS, after starting out at 16, working in the branches counting cash. The mentality there was very entrepreneurial, though. If you delivered, you'd be rewarded, which is how I rose up through the organization. I had plenty of life experience there and, looking back, it was a huge apprenticeship. I was always an entrepreneur and it was in my DNA to go out alone eventually.

Jenny Campbell, CEO, YourCash, and former Dragon

I know what it is like to be a reluctant entrepreneur. Back in 2014, when I first started thinking about Starling Bank, if anyone had said to me, ah, so you are going to be an entrepreneur then, I'd have said 'absolutely not'. I was similarly reluctant to use the word 'founder'.

Growing up, I always believed entrepreneurs were inventors. They *made* something. Today's examples might be James Dyson, because he invented the first bagless vacuum cleaner. Elon Musk invented a rocket that went into space. I didn't believe I was like this. I had gone to university, joined Lloyd's Bank as a graduate trainee and then worked my way up the corporate ladder.

It wasn't until Starling Bank became a unicorn, reaching a valuation of over £1 billion, that I finally relented on the word 'entrepreneur'. Since then, I have reflected on why I never saw myself as a bone fide entrepreneur. My conclusion is that when I started my business, I didn't do it because I wanted to be an entrepreneur. I did it because I had long since grown disillusioned with the world of banking and was convinced that I knew what was needed to be done to put things right. I had zero doubt about my idea for a new type of bank. That, in itself, is the basis for entrepreneurship. What I called myself really didn't matter.

If you too are a reluctant entrepreneur, it might be helpful if I begin by sharing what I, and other female entrepreneurs, think about how to identify whether there is an entrepreneur lurking beneath the surface (whether or not you would like to admit it to yourself).

Ten signs you are an entrepreneur

1. You don't accept 'no' as an answer

Anyone who gets discouraged by a 'no' is never going to make it as an entrepreneur. I held meetings with more than 300 investors before I found someone interested in putting money into Starling Bank. If I had given up at 10 meetings, or a hundred meetings, the business would never have got off the ground. Similarly, plenty of customers, regulators, potential hires, seemingly everyone, said 'no'.

Hearing 'no' time after time is part and parcel of being an entrepreneur. If you are the type to welcome this two-letter word as a challenge that allows you to show what you can do, then you've got the entrepreneur mindset.

2. Your achievements have not been recognized (so far)

Women in particular often get frustrated with corporate life because they feel under-estimated or unrecognized. Their input is ignored or played down. They report speaking up in meetings to put forward an idea and it being met with silence, only for a male colleague to be praised when he repeats a virtually identical point later on. I spent most of my career complaining about not getting the plum projects, or not being paid enough, and very often was only able to make any progress by quitting one job to take another. In the end, I had to start my own business to achieve what I always believed to be my full potential.

It is quite possible that this is the reason why so many women become entrepreneurs following maternity leave. After a break from the corporate world, they can't face re-entering the fray where their achievements go unnoticed month after month. The idea of setting out alone and being judged on their own merits is more alluring.

When I was working for a previous employer, I started thinking, there must be more to life than fixing footnotes on deals that didn't necessarily make a difference to anyone. I ultimately got to a point in the corporate world where I was succeeding, but I didn't feel I was having the impact that I wanted. It was impactful to certain clients, but I wasn't necessarily achieving the full potential of what I could give back to the broader world.

I don't regret having a corporate career first. These were foundational years where I learned useful skill sets, whether it was working with numbers, dealing with clients or communicating effectively. These all gave me a huge leg up. Don't forget also, even though I was out of that setting once I started my business, many of the people I later interacted with as an entrepreneur were still very much in corporate life. It was great to know how they saw the world and the approach they sought.

Romi Savova, Founder and CEO, PensionBee

3. You don't care about fitting in

Closely related to the above, many entrepreneurs have long since decided they don't fit in, so don't waste any time on it. When I started speaking with other female entrepreneurs, I was struck by just how different they were to the people I knew from corporate life. In my previous career, I had been surrounded by people who spent their entire careers trying to fit in. Entrepreneurs didn't seem interested in all of that. They seemed more grounded and focused on the task in hand, rather than carefully weighing each word to see how they came across.

There's an element of mischievousness here, too. It's not enough to feel disgruntled about being passed over; you need to feel determined to do something to strike a blow at the establishment. Any entrepreneur who feels this way would be in fine company. This is the motivation that spurred on Dame Stephanie Shirley, also known as Steve, who started a software house back in 1962 which introduced radical new flexible work practices for women in technology.

I decided to start a business literally overnight. It was not to make money, but as an antidote to the sexism that I found in the workplace. I felt patronized and ignored and wanted my own company to be the sort that I would like to work for and one that lots of other women would like to work for too. It was going to be flexible, honest and straightforward – all the good things in life.

We created a strong culture, employing women with children who could not work in a conventional environment. When equal opportunities legislation came in (Sex Discrimination Act 1975) we had to employ men, and the first few were all disasters. They came in for the wrong reasons and were incompetent. At least we'd kept the plan going for 13 years and it retained its female orientation, with all that implied. We're still all friends now. When we celebrated the 60-year anniversary of the company, 88 people turned up. We definitely broke new ground and that was quite special.

> We did a lot to show women what they could do and what they could aspire to. We also did a lot to show men what women could do.
>
> **Dame Stephanie Shirley, Founder, Freelance Programmers**

4. You're a dreamer (and a little naive)

Entrepreneurs who have previously had 'proper jobs' often report spending a lot of time looking at their firms or bosses and imagining how they would do it better. Their imagination is filled with dreams and ideas.

Mixed in with this is a certain amount of naivety. During my own entrepreneurial journey, it really helped that I dreamed big, but also that I was a little naive about the scale of what I dreamed about. When things were difficult, it helped me imagine the next bit *had to be easier*. I'd tell myself *we only need to get this one thing done and it'll be plain sailing*. This was even though every single day as an entrepreneur is about solving a new problem.

> Entrepreneurs need to be a combination of a huge thinker and a little bit naive. They'll decide to bite off a big problem, I mean a really big problem, such as trying to solve the housing crisis. And you need to tackle problems as big as this to make high-growth businesses, because if you don't think in these terms, there won't be enough of a market to go after. At the same time, if they knew the full ins and outs of the challenge, they'd never do it. That is where the naivety comes in. You somehow convince yourself that you can do it. It's a good combination.
>
> **Alex Depledge, Founder and CEO, Resi**

5. You're competitive

For some reason, a desire to win is often viewed negatively, but it is a quality all entrepreneurs need. In fact, I have not met an entrepreneur who isn't super-competitive. During the toughest times, an arch rival is what you need to keep going, even if that rival doesn't really see your business as a competitor. *They* are the mark. You need to get ahead of them to get closer to your goal. True entrepreneurs turn this rivalry into pure energy.

It should be said, this rivalry should be healthy. Going head-to-head with daggers drawn causes unnecessary tension and doesn't help anyone. New entrepreneurs are often quite surprised to hear that most founders often speak with other businesses in their sector. It's a great way to swap ideas and can help everyone.

6. You're goal-driven

Entrepreneurs are goal-driven. We like to take the initiative and solve problems, even if it means working on them for long periods to remove all obstacles that get in the way. This also means they are strategic in their game plans. Right from the beginning at Starling, I had a grand plan in mind. And it was a *grand* plan. Whenever I talked to anyone about anything to do with the business, I was thinking ahead about how what we were discussing would impact my end goal.

7. You're constantly looking to learn something and improve

Whenever I approach something new, my first instinct is to head to a book-shop. I've been the same ever since I was a young child, when my parents gave me an unlimited budget to spend at our local one. I always bought non-fiction and academic books and would pore over them to find out how to do things. One year, my parents bought me a second-hand, 1956, copy of the *Encyclopaedia Britannica*, all 24 volumes of it. I devoured every page and, perhaps oddly, still have an incredible knowledge of life in the 1950s.

I've never lost the idea that books are there to advise and inform. Whenever I try anything new, I download dozens of books on the subject. If I start something in the house, my kindle is full of books on interior design. My shelves feature a lot of books about living and working in America/Ireland/Switzerland, basically tracking my career progression. Beside them are endless books on starting a business, managing the transition from start-up to high-growth business, or engaging teams (I have included a list of my top recommendations in 'Suggested reading', page 195).

Not everyone is such a bookworm, I understand that. Some gather their intel by meeting as many experts as they can and listening carefully to every word. They learn something from every interaction. Yet, however they absorb it, entrepreneurs are always looking to improve their outlook. If there is a better way to do something, they need to know it.

8. You're good with people

Your employees are people. Your customers are people. Your regulators are people. Your investors are people. *All* of your stakeholders are people. Each one plays a role in making a high-growth business a success. If just one stakeholder doesn't engage, the business won't succeed. Thus, being good with people is key.

9. You're persuasive

To be successful, an entrepreneur needs people to listen to them and be inspired, whether they are investors, customers or colleagues. This talent is essential right from the beginning of an entrepreneurial venture when early team members need to be persuaded to give up the security of their existing jobs to join you on this (potentially crazy) endeavour. When things don't go to plan, you'll have to persuade them to keep the faith and stick with it. Every single difficult conversation has to be sprinkled with just enough magic optimism dust. This is even more so when people are working for next to nothing, or even nothing at all. You need them to come back the next day. Sometimes that takes some next-level charm skills.

Remaining upbeat and persuasive can be particularly challenging during funding rounds, when so much is riding on the outcome. I have many vivid memories of returning to the office empty-handed and yet telling everyone I had a great lead.

10. You're fully committed

Entrepreneurialism is not like an uplifting movie, where the main character has an idea and then a sped-up reel shows them hurtling towards success. There will be multiple high points and low points along the way. Almost every entrepreneur will face a time when they are hours away from losing everything they worked for. Before Starling received its banking licence and began opening accounts, the business came close to collapse three times. It has been well documented that we lost a crucial potential investor at the eleventh hour, and the entire team walked out to start a competitive product (great news, a rival – see point 5 above!). It takes 100 per cent commitment to the vision to keep going at these low points. If you have that, you're an entrepreneur.

Female-led high-growth business entrepreneurs have superpowers too

The characteristics of an entrepreneur largely apply to both male and female entrepreneurs. What's really interesting, though, is that differences also exist between the two genders. And, here is the thing: the specific characteristics of female entrepreneurs can be a *huge* advantage. Despite what the low investment stats seem to show, it turns out female entrepreneurs have many traits that give them a distinct edge over their male counterparts. You could even call them our superpowers.

Take, as an example, the cliché that men find it difficult to multi-task. Like so many of these sayings, there is some truth to this. Women, on the other hand, are good at juggling several tasks at once, while remaining effective and efficient. This is exactly what an entrepreneur needs to do, especially in the early days of a start-up. One of the first lessons of being an entrepreneur is you are entirely responsible for everything that needs to be done. At the beginning, this can be everything from emptying the office waste bins, to registering the company domains, to organizing suppliers and team members, often all at the same time. Something I learned very early on is I can work very efficiently with all sorts of distractions going on nearby. I can sit at my laptop with someone leaning over my shoulder, watching me type, while someone else will be continuing a conversation beside me, while another is asking 'Who wants coffee?'

Multi-tasking may sound like a moot point, with so many other things to think about on the way to building a high-growth business, but that is exactly it. There is tons to do, usually at the same time, and founders need to be on top of it all the time.

Here are some of the other superpowers that put female founders at an advantage:

Intuition

OK, feminine intuition is another cliché but, again, don't dismiss it too quickly. Strong female founders rely heavily on facts and data to make decisions, but they are also excellent at reading those around them. They listen to their instincts when they sense someone on the team is struggling, whether in or out of work, or a project is not developing as it should. This is an invaluable skill when building a business, because things can change rapidly, so it is good to be ahead of the game.

Think of all the angles

Women tend to caretake and curate conversations. During meetings, female founders like to make sure all viewpoints are tackled, even to the point that they will take the opposing viewpoint to their own to debate a point. Their male counterparts, on the other hand, require less information when taking decisions. They tend to take a position and then doggedly hold on to it throughout the debate.

Risk tolerance is an important aspect of entrepreneurialism. While female founders are often accused of being more conservative, there is another side to it. Female founders are more interested in finding the *right* solution, rather than being the person who proposes the *winning* solution. They set aside their ego to make sure the right decision is made.

Value relationships

Female founders tend to value relationships with the team and outside contacts, while male entrepreneurs are more likely to have an approach based on logic. This more emotionally led, social leadership style focuses on listening and understanding where others are coming from, which many people find more authentic and passionate. Passion is the fuel that drives any high-growth business.

> Many people see emotion as a weakness, but some of the biggest deals I have ever done were closed because the other party saw how passionate I was about them. I was with one of our biggest suppliers and we had a big deal on the table. Then, the contact said something about Online4Baby that wasn't true. It caught me off guard and put me on the spot. I had a quick think and regroup, but I had the right answer and showed that we hadn't done what he'd accused us of. I wasn't weeping, but he could see how deeply I felt about what he'd said, and that I was prepared to talk openly about it. He became quite ashamed about it after seeing how important this business and our reputation was to me. That made a big difference. He knew we did things right and he could trust us.
>
> **Christy Foster, Founder, Online4Baby**

Assertive, not aggressive

Many of the female founders I spoke to for this book recalled being labelled 'difficult' at some time or another in their entrepreneurial career. It's an accusation that has been levelled at me a few times, too. I firmly believe this is a badge that should be worn with pride, because it means we are being assertive, which all entrepreneurs need to be. However, it doesn't mean aggressive. Again, this is another communication skill that women excel at. They don't drop hints, or assume people will know what needs to be done. Nor do they throw their weight around, ordering everyone to comply with little explanation why. Female founders are simply open and clear about tasks and what the expectations are. When people don't feel belittled, or on the back foot, they feel respect. This is a far more effective way of unlocking potential.

Self-aware

This superpower is related to the thirst for knowledge discussed earlier. Female founders know their strengths and weaknesses and are not afraid to admit them. If we are not skilled at one aspect of the job, we'll either train ourselves to do it well, or we will find someone who is.

> When I started, I was selling all the time, trying to show how clever I was. Then, I realized I needed someone to help me and he taught me to listen to what other people were saying and to make sure I met their demands.
>
> I made mistakes, too. Early on, I was scared of financial people. I was sure they would come in and ruin the company. We didn't have a finance director for years and my records were kept in a little book. One side of the book was kept for the money coming in and the other for money going out. I was very naive and now see that as absolute madness.
>
> **Dame Stephanie Shirley, Founder, Freelance Programmers**

Are you ready to build a high-growth business?

> I bought a book on how to start a business before I started. I thought it was going to tell me about how to write a business plan. Instead, it began with a bunch of difficult questions like how much money do you earn? What's the minimum you need to live on? What would happen if you earned zero for the next two years?
>
> It isn't enough to have a good idea and be passionate about it. You also need to plan for the downside. There needs to be a Plan B. I'd encourage anyone to go for it, but you need to do it with your eyes open.
>
> **Tania Boler, Founder, Elvie**

If you realize that, yes, you are an entrepreneur at heart and accept that you have many advantages you hadn't previously even considered, there is a decision to be made: do you *want* to be an entrepreneur? Are you truly passionate about building a business that could change everything and make the lives of your customers-to-be infinitely better?

This is a decision not to be taken lightly. Don't be swayed by the potential for wealth and fame (if that is what motivates you). As outlined at the beginning of the chapter, the odds of failure are high. It's not the easiest path. This is the moment to consider what becoming a female founder will mean to you. Will you be happier if you embark on this journey?

When reflecting upon your motivations, there are a number of elements to consider. The first is timing. There is never a perfect time to start a high-growth business. However, you do need to consider how it will impact your personal circumstances. This means your relationships, but it also refers to money. It helps to have a little money behind you, because you will need to eat and pay the bills while on this entrepreneurial adventure. But, and this may sound counter-intuitive, it is best not to have *too much* money. There are entire industries devoted to relieving inexperienced entrepreneurs of their cash. It is very easy to spend money thinking it is helping you to make progress. However, if you have very little spare, you'll be much more likely to scrutinize every decision more carefully. Personal finances are an important consideration, but they shouldn't be a deal breaker.

Consider, also, what else is going on in your life right now. Most entrepreneurs assume their business will be successful in a couple of years and they will exit in five years. The reality is quite different. If it does succeed, and that is a big if, then it can take 10 years or more.

Rates of entrepreneurialism fall sharply among women after the age of 35, which means children must be a consideration for many potential female founders.[7] In most cases, it is a joint decision to have a family, so partners play a role and, all being well, an equal one. Indeed, as Sheryl Sandberg wrote in her book *Lean In*, 'I truly believe that the single most important career decision that a woman makes is whether she will have a life partner and who that partner is.'[8] Even with help, it will be challenging raising young children and growing a business. Sophie Adelman, whose first child was six months old when she started with Multiverse, and who subsequently had another child three years into building the start-up, says conscious trade-offs need to be made.

> It's tough to balance a family and a start-up. I don't want to pull any punches on that. You won't take a lovely long maternity leave. I was on a plane to California to raise money seven weeks after my son was born because that was what needed to be done. You are not going to have the motherhood experience that many of your friends enjoy. You may not even be there to see their first steps.
>
> It is manageable with help, such as nannies and cleaners, and a supportive partner, but you need to accept that you will make those trade-offs and be OK with that.
>
> **Sophie Adelman, Co-Founder, Multiverse and One Garden**

Another concern is how the eco system around high-growth businesses views female founders who start families while scaling. In particular, this means investors who are making the decisions about whether to back these firms. The world has, thankfully, moved on a long way and there are robust maternity protections for women in the workplace. However, it has not been unheard of for investors to openly question female founders about their intentions when it comes to children, or their decision to have them. This somehow manages to slip through a loophole in the law. While the Financial Conduct Authority regulates investors, there is no *employment contract* between the various parties, so discriminatory comments can slip through with little recourse. Fortunately, this is becoming rarer and the majority of VCs take a more enlightened approach. Again, awareness and open discussion is key.

> We can't just pretend it won't happen. We need to start to talk about it more openly. This way we can better navigate the issue and ensure that everyone can start and grow companies. Entrepreneurship is not just a thing for certain people who have huge amounts of money and privilege, together with zero responsibilities.
>
> It's really important to acknowledge that women are the ones who give birth after carrying their babies for nine months and then are very involved in the first months with breastfeeding. It's a huge deal and just factually much more impactful for the person carrying and birthing the child. We absolutely cannot just equate parents who are not pregnant and don't give birth and women who do to having the same role in that process. It's something that, if we don't talk about it more often, is going to be a taboo subject and entrepreneurs will just feel they can't bring it up with funders, or perhaps even start a company at all.

It is possible to lead a high-growth business *and* have children. It's completely compatible. We've had multiple founders in our portfolio, both men and women, who have had kids and taken parental leave whilst going through seed rounds or while scaling up their businesses. It's incumbent on the VC to do much more to support founders doing this. To give an example of what my team at Ada Ventures did for me when I had my own child, they gave me £2,000 of childcare credits as a company benefit. I used it to pay for a night nanny, which was amazing and meant I could get back to work much more quickly. This was a tangible, meaningful intervention that my company made, which made my journey as a mother and a leader so much easier. There are lots of other tangible things that companies and VCs can do to make the journey easier for female founders with children.

Check Warner, Co-Founder and Partner, Ada Ventures

For a high-growth business to have a chance of success, the timing has to be right in both the market itself and from a personal point of view. Once female founders feel they have the right idea, they can do themselves some favours by pausing to validate that they are personally ready.

The final motivation is closely linked to the subject of the next chapter, and that is the business you want to create. Is your idea driven by a sense of mission and purpose, a desire to make the world a better place? Or do you just want to be your own boss? The former is a much stronger reason to start a high-growth business, and the passion for it will sustain you through the tough times. When I set up Starling Bank, I wanted to start a business that had huge impact and was going to break boundaries. I didn't think about the personal benefits.

In this chapter, we've talked a lot about the positive qualities, even super-powers, that might make you a perfect entrepreneur. But, if you know yourself well, you will understand that you do have some personality traits that can also hold you back. You might be averse to uncertainty, or dislike change. You may even be a perfectionist. How will these characteristics impact your journey to create a high-growth business?

If you consider all of this and still have a burning desire to build a high-growth business, that's great news. Now, you just need to get on with it.

The biggest step forward is just to do it. It is natural to be plagued by fears of failing, or not knowing really where to start. It can be paralysing. There's a stereotype that women tend to take less risk and, in some cases, we are encouraged to stick with the safe options.

If you feel like this, get started by taking a series of small steps, such as buying domain names, registering the company and so on. Even if each step is small, each one will help you gain confidence. People spend too long analysing how exactly to do it and do nothing because they overthink it instead of getting going and moving forward.

Check Warner, Co-Founder and Partner, Ada Ventures

Notes

[1] Beahurst. Top 200 women-powered businesses, Beahurst and JP Morgan, 2023. assets. jpmprivatebank.com/content/dam/jpm-wm-aem/other/top-200-uk/Top200_Women-Powered_ Businesses_2023.pdf (archived at https://perma.cc/7XKE-3HLF)

[2] A Bacon. Less than 1% of €50m+ rounds went to all-female founding teams last year, Sifted, 13 June 2023. sifted.eu/articles/sista-bcg-gender-diversity-report-news (archived at https:// perma.cc/F7YK-LVTM)

[3] A Bacon. Less than 1% of €50m+ rounds went to all-female founding teams last year, Sifted, 13 June 2023. sifted.eu/articles/sista-bcg-gender-diversity-report-news (archived at https:// perma.cc/F7YK-LVTM)

[4] SheCanCode. Female-founded tech startups are defying downward trends, SheCanCode, 8 June 2023. shecancode.io/blog/female-founded-tech-startups-are-defying-downward-trends (archived at https://perma.cc/9MZN-Y8BB)

[5] K Abouzahr, M Krentz, J Harthorne and F Brooks Taplett. Why women-owned startups are a better bet, BCG, 6 June 2018. www.bcg.com/publications/2018/why-women-owned-startups-are-better-bet (archived at https://perma.cc/25TU-BZ3K)

[6] Court of Arbitration of the European Chamber of Digital Commerce. Statistics show women are better entrepreneurs than men, Court of Arbitration of the European Chamber of Digital Commerce, 16 June 2019. europeanchamberofdigitalcommerce.com/statistics-show-women-are-better-entrepreneurs-than-men (archived at https://perma.cc/DB7W-XURX)

[7] A Rose. The Alison Rose review of female entrepreneurship, 2019. assets.publishing.service. gov.uk/government/uploads/system/uploads/attachment_data/file/784324/RoseReview_ Digital_FINAL.PDF (archived at https://perma.cc/Z5GL-4LWS)

[8] S Sandberg (2015) *Lean In: Women, work, and the will to lead*, WH Allen, London

CHAPTER TWO

The big idea

The origin for many high-growth business ideas is seeing something that doesn't work as it should and coming up with a better way. This was the basis for Starling Bank. After many years working for traditional banks, I could see banking was broken. High street banks were not working in the interests of account holders, not even close, and everyone seemed to know it except banks themselves. That is what spurred me on to build a customer-first digital bank. Occasionally, these light bulb moments come as a result of a single experience. Romi Savova moved from her corporate career with Morgan Stanley to the start-up Credit Benchmark after deciding to pursue a different sort of career. Transferring her pensions as part of the move should have been an easy task, but the experience was, in her words, 'harrowing'. She realized what she'd been through was not unique. Millions of people must have felt similar frustration at the complexity of the admin around moving pensions and, inevitably, pension funds would get lost or forgotten about. This was the genesis for the idea of PensionBee.

In both cases, we were pursuing a business disruption model, where we sought to replace the traditional products and services in our markets with a new and infinitely more efficient alternative. Also, in both cases, tech was at the centre of the disruptive model. One of the earliest examples of this was lastminute.com, co-founded by Martha Lane Fox in 1998 during the so-called dot-com boom. Before then, the holiday sector was built around high street travel agents who would promote deals via postcards in their windows, or Teletext. Most of the best deals were for trips that were just days away, hence the deep discounts. Lastminute.com scooped-up this unsold inventory and sold it online. There was something in the new model for everyone. Tour companies cut their losses by disposing of trips that hadn't sold, and customers received attractive discounts, all delivered by a smart online service with cheeky branding to emphasize the holiday mood.

The key to successfully building a high-growth business is finding an idea that will *scale*. Scaling is where revenue rises *without* substantial increases in costs. If the only way to scale is to expand physically, and add on more resources, the business will forever be stuck in a holding pattern. Think here of a care home. For such a business to expand, it will need to add more bedrooms to accommodate more residents, which in turn will also require more staff to look after those residents. Yes, the strategy will bring in further income, but it will also come with a substantial added cost. It will, therefore, not be a high-growth business. This is linear growth, where a company adds on new resources, whether it is capital, people or technology, and revenue increases as a result of this investment.

In the past, one of the reasons put forward as to why there are less female-founded high-growth businesses is that women are more naturally drawn to ideas where they can make a social contribution, and gravitate to 'people-focused' businesses.[1] These enterprises are traditionally labour intensive and therefore not scalable. This preference appears to be reflected in the statistics, too. In 2022, 37 per cent of fashion/wellness start-ups were founded by all-female teams, as were 24 per cent of lifestyle businesses and 18 per cent in healthcare. In comparison, among the less labour-intensive fintech sector, just 7 per cent of start-ups were all-female led.[2] We do, however, need to look beyond the raw numbers. Many of the most successful female-led enterprises are indeed in these areas, but a growing number have found a way to scale. They've done so by making full use of technology.

Tania Boler is a pioneer in healthtech, or female-first technology as she calls it. Her business Elvie has developed a range of health and lifestyle products to tackle intimate issues impacting women. Since its launch in 2013, Elvie has grown to be a £100 million business on the back of high-tech developments such as silent breast pumps and an app-synched pelvic floor trainer.

> My original idea for the business was based around a service model where we would go into people's homes and help them with pelvic floor exercises. I spent four months working on it and then someone come in to advise me from

a commercial viewpoint and he told me there was no way this was going to work. It wouldn't scale. I was completely heartbroken. But, he was right. That was when I shifted to technology. I was passionate about the issue of pelvic floor health, but this was the only way to make the proposition work.

It is tough when people rip your ideas apart, but the only way to develop them is to subject them to scrutiny. You need to view them through a commercial lens.

Tania Boler, Founder, Elvie

Another good example of tech-fuelled high growth in the healthcare sector is Portman Dental Care. This business is one I am very familiar with, since my own dentist was one of the first dentists to join the business and she is now a non-executive director. The marketing for the business, which has been named as Outstanding Business of the Year at the British Dentistry Awards for a number of consecutive years, makes much of its 'patient focus'. There are 200 dental practices across the UK, Ireland and Benelux, caring for over 700,000 patients and, yes, the service is excellent, thanks to both skilled practitioners and state-of-the art equipment at each practice. What makes it a high-growth business, though, is the centralized digital platform which drives it. Rather than 200 separate dentist platforms, it is run as one big business, sharing a central infrastructure such as booking systems and training.

It is highly likely that in the months and years to come, other social sectors which were traditionally tough to scale will experience a boom in more tech-orientated start-ups. Certainly, we are already seeing a huge amount of growth in so-called climate-tech and the UK is leading the way in Europe for the number of climate-tech companies.[3] With impatience growing at the apparently slow response to rising temperatures by governments around the globe and failures to implement meaningful change, there has been a spate of start-up innovations devoted towards achieving net zero. These female-led climate-tech start-ups are tackling the issue from a number of angles. Moria Zituny Bennett founded Tevva Motors, which produces electric trucks designed to do the heavy duty work of a diesel truck without the environmental impact. Smol, co-founded by Paula Quazi, is tackling plastic waste with eco-cleaning ranges for dishes and laundry available via online subscription. Meanwhile, Edinburgh start-up Earth Blox, led by Genevieve Patenaude, is using satellite data to identify deforestation or mining activities and monitor supply chains.

There has been a marked growth in food-tech start-ups, too, where we're seeing innovations in a range of spaces, from vegan start-ups that are hoping to tempt consumers away from meat by producing lab-made alternatives, to ones dealing with food waste. Too Good To Go, a pan-European app launched by Mette Lykke, partners with more than 50,000 supermarkets, restaurants, bakeries and hotels to make up 'Magic Bags' of surplus food items that remain unsold, which can be purchased via the app. DnaNudge, founded by Maria Karvela, combines foodtech and healthtech using wearable technology to guide consumers away from food that could cause them illnesses they might be prone to, such as type 2 diabetes.

Technology is not an automatic win in the high-growth stakes, even if it is great tech, but it does feature in the majority of fast-growing businesses in this sector. It should also be said that it is possible for a start-up to showcase the absolute best technology, but if nobody is willing to pay for it, then it is not going to become a high-growth business. Sometimes, the market is just not ready for an idea, or it is not seen as a commercial proposition.

Solve problems that exist

How, then, do you settle on the big idea that has the potential to scale? The obvious starting point is the same one the chapter began with, which is to find a problem that needs solving. This will be far more productive than beginning with a burning desire to be the next Amazon, or SpaceX. Instead of starting from existing companies and working back to the problem they solve, seek out problems and imagine how your start-up might solve them.

It can be a helpful exercise to look around you and ask yourself what you would like someone else to develop to make your life better. It could well be something that's been bugging you for a while. *If there was x, this product/ service would work as it should.* Make sure it is a problem that you passionately feel needs to be addressed too. If you start a business, you may well be working towards solving it for the next decade. To dedicate this much time and energy to something, you need to feel fully invested in it.

This was one of the tests for Sophie Adelman. Sophie, together with Euan Blair, launched WhiteHat (later named Multiverse) with the mission of 'democratizing access to the best careers'. The core idea was to offer an alternative to university by recruiting and training young people as apprentices at some of the world's best companies.

> The idea really resonated with me because I could see that this was a problem that needed solving in society and it was something that I had personal experience of too. While I was very academic, I had a lot of friends for whom university was not the right path. It seemed insane to me that the wider world thinks it is university or bust. The timing was particularly pertinent because it costs so much more to attend university today and the government had recently announced the introduction of an apprenticeship levy on companies. This created an opportunity to encourage companies to consider apprenticeships to build their talent pipeline.
>
> I feel strongly about levelling the playing field so ambitious kids from all backgrounds have another path to follow that is as prestigious as the best universities.
>
> **Sophie Adelman, Co-Founder, Multiverse and One Garden**

It is very easy to get hung up on the thought that an idea has to be unique. Don't. In fact, it is very rare to come up with a completely new concept. In the case of Multiverse, there were already a large number of apprenticeship providers in the UK, many of which were supplying a volume of opportunities in the market. What needs to stand out is the *solution* being offered.

> What we did didn't involve completely reinventing the wheel. Yes, thousands of apprenticeships happened each year, but the process didn't work very well. The solutions on offer didn't serve the needs of employers, the administrative element was poorly handled and the branding was terrible. What we did was to ask ourselves: how can we do this 10 times better than everyone else and then take it forward and make it 10 times better than what universities were offering? How can we use technology, initially to facilitate the process, and ultimately to transform the experience, without losing the human element? We always remembered we were focused on changing people's lives and put that at the heart of our offering.
>
> **Sophie Adelman, Co-Founder, Multiverse and One Garden**

The Multiverse solution had three main elements; a digital marketplace matching candidate profiles with potential opportunities, access to high-quality coaching and outstanding educational resources, and an apprentice community that emulated the social side of university life.

If the market already seems saturated with players, it's a natural reaction to rush back to the drawing board to think of something else. But, as long as the new solution on offer is sufficiently different and compelling, a crowded existing market can be a good thing. In fact, it can really help during investment rounds. Investors feel more comfortable when there are competitors, because it's a handy way to create benchmarks around what is good or bad, and what works or doesn't, all of which is vital information when it comes to analysing new propositions. This stands whether or not the incumbents are traditional players who have served the market for decades, or other start-ups who have also spotted that there is a better way of doing things. If a new wave of disruption is already gaining traction, it is a sure sign that this is an interesting sector. Investors will be curious to take a look at all the players and make their own judgement about which solutions will eventually come out on top.

We were alone in our market for the first seven years. In some ways, this is great for a first mover advantage, but then you also get the situation where investors ask: why is no one else doing this? We had to explain over and over that the large incumbents weren't all that keen on dealing with consumers directly, whereas we were.

We were correct in our timing, though. When I began to think about pensions, I knew most people found the subject a bit boring. However, the idea of online consumer financial services was just beginning to take hold. TransferWise (now Wise) had launched not that long before. When I first heard about Wise, I thought, I am not going to use some online service for money. Then I saw a billboard advertising it and I realized that this is the way things were going. When I met my co-founder Jonathan (Lister Parsons, PensionBee's Chief Technology Officer) and he told me he'd had a similar horrible experience to me when transferring his pension. I thought, we really have to do this. Everything had come together and pointed to the fact that this could work.

You can have amazing ideas, but if they are before their time, they won't get traction because the appetite won't be there. That doesn't mean you can't revisit them later.

Romi Savova, Founder and CEO, PensionBee

There is another advantage to entering an established market too – start-ups can learn a lot from their competitors. Why waste time and money on making your own mistakes, or on costly research and focus groups, when you can see what other businesses in your sector get wrong?

Luck or timing, or a bit of both

Industry transformations tend to come in waves. If a business idea comes *too early* in the wave, then founders will find it very difficult indeed to raise money, because investors won't understand what it is they are looking at. Even if they do appreciate the concept, they'll be wary about backing something that is so untried and untested. It will be almost impossible to raise funding. There is also a stage where it is simply *too late*. I still regularly get requests for mentoring and support from entrepreneurs with an eye on setting up a neo bank. The time to become the next Starling Bank, Monzo or Revolut has long passed. A small handful of challenger banks have already made a huge impact and captured a significant number of consumers who were fed up with traditional banks and longing for something better. If there are already a number of dominant players in the market, there is no point setting up something else that is largely similar. Once the battle has been won, it has been won. Entrepreneurs need to part of a wave for it to be attractive to investors. However, they must be close to the *beginning* of a wave, although not too far out in front, but definitely not lagging a long way behind.

My father was an entrepreneur and my biggest role model. When I was very young, he told me that one day there would be a phone with a video attached, so we could see who we are talking to. In those days, we had phones with a rotary dial, and when you called to speak with someone in another country, you needed to go via an operator and could only speak for three minutes. Such an idea seemed so far away from what we had then. Even if the technology had been available, it would have been a really hard sell.

Even just 15 years ago, what would you have said if I told you that you would climb into a stranger's car to get a lift somewhere? Yet, today, Uber and Lyft are the norm. It's all innovation but, to get the commercial aspect right, timing is crucial.

Deepali Nangia, Partner, Female and Diverse Founders, Speedinvest

When it comes to timing, sometimes, there is an element of luck involved, too. When I first began to think about Starling in 2014 (then known as New Bank), we were firmly at the beginning of the wave of bank industry innovation. At that time, there were just two other so-called neo banks, Atom and Tandem, and we'd all declared our intention to challenge the status quo of traditional banking. I was around six weeks into the planning process, speaking with as many people as I could, when a good contact complimented me on my perfect timing. Unsure of how to respond, yet unwilling to admit I didn't quite understand the comment, I pretended that, yes, my timing was exquisite. It's only when he casually mentioned 'loosening regulations' that I cottoned on to what he was talking about but, even then, I was a bit mystified.

Once I'd finished the meeting, I did some hurried Google searches and then fully understood why my timing was, indeed, so spot on. Banking regulations had very recently changed to encourage competition in the sector, as a result of political efforts to inject competition into banking. The so-called 'big four' banks, Barclays, Lloyds, HSBC and Royal Bank of Scotland were seen to be just too dominant, controlling 77 per cent of the personal current account market. This was deemed a situation that could not continue in the aftermath of the 2008 financial crisis.[4] Despite my lengthy career in banking, these regulatory developments had not been on my radar. Thus, although my timing was indeed good, there was an element of luck involved too. Looking back, I wonder what I would have done if the regulations had not been changed. Would I have succeeded in getting the rules changed? I suspect not. Not easily, anyhow. It would have taken many years and it was quite likely I would have run out of money long before I succeeded.

If the timing seems good, the next step is to explore whether there is an appetite/market for the business concept you've decided upon. Some knowledge of the sector and a little desk research will reveal the basics about the main players, the size of the total addressable market (TAM) and the profile of the most active customers. Yet, how do you find out if customers will want the product or service you want to launch? You know that you feel strongly about it and are passionate that this concept is needed, but what if you are alone in this?

The answer is to develop a minimum viable product (MVP) and put it to the test.

Test the idea with real potential customers

After I first came up with my idea for a new type of bank and resigned from my day job, I decided to take some time away to work it all through. It was billed as a holiday, since I'd booked myself onto a cruise around South Africa, but I had a long 'to do' list in my head. Sunbathing and reading trashy novels was not on that agenda. I didn't even take my usual large pile of business books, which I love to unwind with. My plan was to scrutinize each of the apps that were then available from the main banks and to write a detailed review of each one, highlighting what I thought worked, what didn't and what might work given some improvement. On day one of the cruise, I ditched the plan. Instead, I went out to talk to real people, those who used the apps, to find out what they did and didn't like about them. What they told me was far more useful than a slightly clinical review I'd planned to carry out.

When starting a new business, particularly one with a large tech element, it is very easy to pontificate. Entrepreneurs can become fixated with building the all-singing, all-dancing platform they've dreamed about, before showing it to anyone. An element of this is they don't want anyone else to steal the idea. They also might believe it is such a complex undertaking, it will be far better to present customers with a fait accompli. *Tah dah, look at this brilliant solution to the problem that has been plaguing you for years!*

There is so much wrong with this plan. To begin with, there is the *assumption* that the problem being solved does bother others immeasurably. In reality, they might be perfectly happy with the status quo. If that does turn out to be the case, and customers are indifferent to the launch of the product, imagine how much money will have been wasted building that perfect solution, which turned out to be not so perfect after all. As for keeping everything confidential, forget it. As outlined above, it is very rare to come up with an entirely new idea. The secret sauce, the thing that will, all being well, create a gravity-defying high-growth business is in the team behind it and the execution. No one can copy that.

Once an entrepreneur has an idea they believe works, they need to get it out into the market in its rawest form and test it. Do the absolute basics of the plan and execute fast. Start to build *something*, however simple, that people can give you feedback on. There is no point in spending huge amounts of time and money on drawing up hypothetical designs and plotting out business plans without getting feedback from the market. You could be going in completely the wrong direction and need to totally change your strategy.

One of the issues I see a lot in the UK, certainly more so than in the USA, is we overthink things. We write detailed plans of everything we are going to do and spend weeks going over and over them to get them just right. What we should

---

really be doing is just making a start. But getting started doesn't necessarily mean diving in to do things you don't need to do yet.

Because I'm in the tech business, everyone assumes that when I say get started, it means writing code. That is the worst thing you can do when you can test the idea manually. Say you wanted to build an online marketplace for children's parties. Eager to get on with it, you may speak with web designers and coders, briefing them to map out the transaction process and begin building the website. What anyone in this position *should* be doing is seeking out about a dozen or so providers of children's party services in their local area and then having a go at matching them with the target customer. This would mean physically going along to a local school, or playgroup, at home time and asking the parents there if they are interested in children's party services. If that exercise works, and they are all eager to learn more about this new offer, then you can start thinking about building the website.

When we started Resi, we put an ad on Facebook asking people if they were looking for local architects. When people clicked on it, we said we'd be back in touch. We wanted to gauge the size of the market and to see what language attracted people.

There are a lot of ways to smoke test ideas and they don't involve jumping in to do the costliest thing, which is building a digital version. Whatever the business model, start building it in the physical world first.

Alex Depledge, Founder and CEO, Resi

Finding a quick and simple way to test a complex tech idea might seem challenging. After all, writing code for a fully functional product can take thousands of man hours, which comes at a huge cost. There is, however, a way to test products before getting to the coding stage. To explain this, let's use the example of a fictional artificial intelligence (AI) interface that will help households through the cost-of-living crisis. The idea of the app is that it automatically switches households between sustainable energy sources, be it wind turbines, heat pumps, or solar, according to which one is generating the most at that particular moment, thus saving considerably on power bills.

The first step might be to send out a blank email to 1,000 would-be consumers of this new app. Yes, a blank email. The subject header for the email could be something like: 'Optimize your energy at home.' If no one opens the email, it's because it's not pitched right. No one understands what it means, or they do not perceive that it solves their problem. The next step is to send out another blank email, this one with the header: 'Save £1000 a year on your energy bills'. If half of the recipients open the email, the entrepreneur is most likely onto something. This is the time to take it to the next stage.

In this third step, the entrepreneur would build a basic website allowing customers to key in information about the size of their house, where they live and other basic details. The promise on offer is that these details will enable the bespoke AI to provide an answer to how much the household can save each year by connecting to and then alternating between the providers of wind, air and solar sources signed up to the app. The 'bespoke AI' will be nothing more than the most basic of basic websites. There will be no miraculous machine-learning function built into the back end. The calculation will be carried out by someone in the office, who will do the research and calculations manually after customers have keyed in their information.

These simple steps test the market to see if there is an appetite. The basic website won't be perfect. It will be a long, long way from what the all-singing, all-dancing end product will look like and won't be able to do a fraction of what it would be able to do when built. In fact, it will be downright scrappy. However, it will provide invaluable feedback on whether there is an appetite for the service and how customers will use it.

This primary goal of a process like this is to test out whether there is an appetite for the idea, but the feedback that comes with it will be invaluable too. The 'test panel' may agree that there is a problem with a particular market and welcome a solution. However, they may not welcome the solution under discussion. At least, not in its present form. There is no necessity to take every suggestion on board, but some may lead to useful changes in the core offer. This is a process that any entrepreneur should get used to. While the problem will stay the same, the solution will constantly evolve. New suggestions will come in all the time, too. Early tweaks can come from this test phase, and then again as an entrepreneur begins to build their team and hires in specialists. During investment rounds, VCs and angels will almost inevitably suggest improvements. Again, these people are worth listening to, because they are experienced in the market and know what works. This process will be repeated when the product finally gets into the hands of customers too. The users will have input over what features they like and don't like. It's always wise to listen to this feedback and adjust accordingly.

The real high-growth potential might not be in the first idea you had when you set out. A lot of companies start life as, say, a software business, and they end up as a data company. The founders discover that there is more value in their data than in the software they've built. If others want access to that data, it makes more sense to monetize the data. This could mean you may build a company that you weren't planning on building. It's the mark of true entrepreneurial talent to not be fixated on the original idea and to follow the opportunity.

Zandra Moore, Founder and CEO, Panintelligence

Notes

[1] A Bin Shmailan. Compare the characteristics of male and female entrepreneurs as explorative study, *Journal of Entrepreneurship & Organization Management*, 5 (4), 2016. www.hilarispublisher.com/open-access/compare-the-characteristics-of-male-and-female-entrepreneurs-as-explorative-study-2169-026X-1000203.pdf (archived at https://perma.cc/47M3-6P9F)

[2] A Bacon. Less than 1% of €50m+ rounds went to all-female founding teams last year, Sifted, 13 June 2023. sifted.eu/articles/sista-bcg-gender-diversity-report-news (archived at https://perma.cc/F7YK-LVTM)

[3] Just Entrepreneurs. 32 revolutionary climate tech companies, Just Entrepreneurs, 14 October 2022. justentrepreneurs.co.uk/news/32-revolutionary-climate-tech-companies (archived at https://perma.cc/56TT-5EMX)

[4] E Dunkley. 'Challenger' banks try to shake up big four, *Financial Times*, 4 January 2015. www.ft.com/content/d2520afa-8b78-11e4-ae73-00144feabdc0 (archived at https://perma.cc/Z6Y5-CDGP)

CHAPTER THREE

Leveraging skills, experience and contacts

There's a world of difference between having a great idea and achieving unicorn status. No matter how brilliant the timing, or how passionate and committed the entrepreneur, supercharging a business to propel it into high growth is quite the challenge. Going it alone is not always the best option, which is why entrepreneurs need to make a good range of contacts.

One of the best-known ways to get started in this endeavour is via accelerators and incubators. These programmes help start-ups quickly get established and scale up. During my own fundraising journey, I met several investors who asked whether I had applied to an accelerator. The not-very-subtle subtext to this question was that if I had not, I couldn't have been very serious about my business. *Does this founder think they are so special they don't need any help and advice?*

I did spend time at one accelerator, which was run by Google, but it was not until around three years after starting Starling. My motivation was simple; like all accelerators, it represented an opportunity to network with high-calibre organizations that might be helpful to start-ups, in this case Capital G. It was run over three separate weeks, which was short by accelerator standards, and was based around machine learning. Did I find it a useful exercise? If I am honest, I learned some things but I am not convinced it was worth three weeks of my time.

Let's, though, begin with the basics. At face value, accelerators and incubators look like two very different options. Accelerators are generally three- to six-month programmes that are usually only open to start-ups that already have a minimum viable product and a team in place. Incubators, on the other hand, tend to take on entrepreneurs at an earlier ideas stage, and work with them on a longer timeframe which can stretch beyond two years. When it comes to funding, accelerators will often provide seed funding right from the start, in exchange for equity, while, with incubators funding opportunities often come at the end of the programme. Incubators may, however, ask for equity in exchange for the networking opportunities, mentoring and office space they provide.

In reality, the lines between accelerators and incubators are much less well defined. Indeed, many organizations bill themselves as both and offer a hybrid of the models outlined in the above paragraph. The best-known are Y Combinator, Techstars and Entrepreneur First, but there are many, many more around the world, in a mix of virtual, hybrid and in-person programmes (a number can be found in 'Further information', page 189). They can be run by a mix of corporations or venture capital firms, or are government-led or university sponsored programmes, or set up by large corporates.

Many accelerators/incubators focus on a specific sector, such as healthcare, or technology that promises to improve the outlook for the planet. There are also a number that particularly welcome applications from female-led businesses. It's worth spending some time researching the most appropriate one.

I was quite lucky that PwC badgered me to join their accelerator programme. Or, to be exact, the guy running it said: 'I need to get a female on this programme otherwise I'm going to get my ass kicked.' I had to laugh at that. He wasn't exactly making me feel special.

The programme was brilliant because I did learn a lot and it was really good for me. It especially helped by introducing me into the advisor networks. I'm from a working-class family and the first entrepreneur in the family. There wasn't a pot of money behind me and no one in my family has ever raised money for a business before. I'd basically emptied my savings to buy the IP for my business, and used what I had to grow and scale it. What this also meant was that I didn't have that network of people to lean on and advise me. The accelerator changed that and helped me establish that network.

Zandra Moore, Founder and CEO, Panintelligence

The central idea around accelerators and incubators is to give entrepreneurs contacts and confidence. Many pure accelerator programmes are an intense, immersive experience and founders can expect to meet experienced entrepreneurs who will drop by to tell their own inspiring story, as well as investors and leaders of more traditional firms. Learning-by-doing is key to the experience and founders should be prepared to find many years of learning compressed into an intense period. The culmination of the programme is Demo Day, where fledgling entrepreneurs demonstrate what they've built to a roomful of potential investors.

The pure incubator model is generally more suited to smaller businesses that don't harbour ambitions for high growth in the very near future, since their focus is not on helping businesses scale. Their remit is more to help entrepreneurs hone their business idea and support them as they develop it. The resources and services on offer vary, but might include access to office space at below market rates, mentorship opportunities, networking events and classes on specific aspects of founding and running a start-up. Starting up any business can be a lonely and daunting experience. By joining an incubator, entrepreneurs will be surrounded by other people going through the exact same thing. This can be a source of networking opportunities or simply a chance to let off some steam with others experiencing the same challenges. There will also be a range of mentors available who can help guide founders, as well as access to equipment and admin resources.

Signing up may seem like a big commitment at this stage, even with a pure accelerator which offers programmes compacted into a few months. This is especially so when an entrepreneur is keen to get on with starting then growing their business. The strongest argument in their favour is in the numbers. Start-ups that have attended accelerators have strong survival rates, with 79 per cent that were signed up to the UK's top accelerators surviving their third anniversary, versus 40 per cent who achieved this milestone without help.[1] The odds of getting investment are also higher, with 55 per cent of accelerated start-ups successful in their fundraising. However, it should be noted that just 3 per cent raised over £40 million.

The most important thing to note here is: not all accelerators and incubators are the same. The odds of these positive outcomes are improved if entrepreneurs work with the best-performing accelerators. There are other potential downsides, too. Take as an example the accelerators/incubators set up by large corporates. These big organizations invariably try to show off their entrepreneurial credentials by locating these services in the grittier end of town. The 'casual and creative' décor will be designed around bare-brick walls, brightly coloured bean bags and top-notch, chrome-tapped espresso makers, with the ensemble only slightly spoiled by a smattering of less chic, clunky office chairs that are clearly on loan from the parent organization. The most significant issue, though, might be the affiliation with the corporate. Take an aspiring fintech start-up, which signs up to an accelerator/incubator run by Barclays Bank. Do you think this link with the high-street bank will reduce the chances that, say, Lloyds would buy the business after it 'graduated'? I think it very well might.

Accelerators and incubators vary, but some do have a definite edge to them too. It's rather like being back at school, where the cool kids thrive but anyone who doesn't quite look like everyone else stands out as a bit awkward/different. As a woman over 50, from a corporate background, I was always in the latter category. Other female founders may find they feel the same. There is also a discernible hierarchy among start-ups according to their valuations, i.e. those with the highest valuations are 'top dog'.

There are cost implications tied up in this, too, which can be daunting for a founder who is already living off their savings to get their business started. (By cost, I mean expenses, rather than paying for an accelerator. In all cases, founders should follow the tried-and-tested start-up route and never pay for anything. I even managed to get my flights paid for – and upgraded – on the accelerator I attended.) Think, too, about the time factor. Even if you attend one close to home, there will be many meetings, coaching sessions and other potential distractions that will eat into the time needed to get a start-up off the ground. Joining an accelerator or incubator means actively engaging with others in the community and, while it is nice to find common ground, other early-stage entrepreneurs are not necessarily the ecosystem they need. Someone once said to me that you don't get a job by hanging around with people who don't have a job. The same goes in the world of entrepreneurialism. If you want to found a high-growth business, you need to hang around with founders who are already well into their journey. Finally, there is the early loss of equity involved, which can be daunting, particularly when there are no guarantees that the business will succeed after the programme. While there is a huge amount to be said for accelerators and incubators, they are not for everyone.

Perhaps my biggest issue with the format, though, is that entrepreneurs are expected to be present and correct all the time. This includes going out on visits to various entrepreneurs to hear their 'how-I-did-it' talks. I have never been one to want to stick to a strict timetable, much preferring getting around, talking to people informally and doing three things at once. Plus, I have never seen a whole lot of value in hearing about, say, how an entrepreneur launched a high-tech vineyard when I was trying to start a bank.

It is, of course, a personal decision. Entrepreneurs who do decide that there is some value to working with accelerators/incubators are advised to choose the programme carefully, to make sure the model is suited to the needs of their business. They should be prepared that the application process is rigorous and will require extensive information about the business, product, market and team. These applications will be assessed in detail before candidates are interviewed and evaluated, and competition is fierce for the best known.

Networking

One aspect of the entrepreneur support ecosystem that cannot be ignored is networking. Networking is the tried and tested route to strengthen business connections, and all entrepreneurs need a rock-solid network. It's not just about raising a personal profile, although this will be crucial as they proceed through the high-growth journey. Founders need to surround themselves with people who have the skills they'll need to draw upon. The right connections are crucial.

This can present a problem for women entrepreneurs in particular. Networking events, particularly in male-dominated industries, are often frequented almost solely by men. Female founders should prepare themselves that there is a high possibility that they will be the only woman in the room, and people may be sceptical about what they have to say. Strange though it might sound, some men are uncomfortable about engaging with women in these situations, meaning it can be a challenge to engage in a relaxing and potentially mutually beneficial conversation.

Even our physical attributes can put us at a disadvantage. In an event where one is expected to stand and mingle, many women will spend the entire event with neck ache as they look up at the other networkers in order to engage. I know this from bitter experience as a person who is not much more than five feet tall. This puts women at an entirely different level right from the start, in every way. Plus, it makes it almost impossible to break into a conversation among a group of a dozen or more tall people. They really don't look down.

The alternative might be to create one's own mini networking situations, by inviting potentially key contacts out for a drink and a chat. Even this is fraught with danger, though. Even in a business environment, it's still unusual for a woman to invite a man for a drink, whether it is with a view to making them an offer to join a team, or to ask for advice.

An obvious solution is to join networking organizations that specialize in female entrepreneurs, or ones that run certain events specifically for female founders. In the latter category, I found the occasional women-only networking dinners organized by The Up Group particularly useful in this respect.[2] These were aimed at women in tech and very accessible. Before each event, the names of attendees are sent out and it is possible to request a place seated beside a particular contact. You can request a few, because attendees are required to move seats after each course. I would, however, advise against refining networking efforts to only ever attending female-only events. Such forums can limit the range of people female founders are exposed to, when the aim of the process is to broaden their network as far as possible. Events are also more likely to be attended by other early-stage female-led businesses, because successful female founders are more likely to be found at larger, more 'mainstream' events, if they have time to attend them at all. As highlighted in the accelerator/incubators section, there is not always a great deal of value spending a large amount of time with other founders at the same stage, whether or not they are female. These events can be useful, but the advice is to choose carefully.

Some events are so good for networking, you might need to take a bold and unusual approach. I once attended the annual exhibition at the Royal Society of Arts for three evenings over a space of 10 days. There was a different group of people there each time, many in the field of investment, banking and executive search. It took a bit of stamina, but I made some useful contacts and no one knew I had been there night after night.

To reap the full benefits of networking, the only realistic solution is for female founders to adopt strategies to not only feel comfortable attending mixed networking events, but also to come away from them with a good range of strong contacts. One strategy to get over the awkwardness is to take along a wing man or woman, which will take away the problem of having to plunge into a room full of people who all seem to know each other.

Most events I go to are attended by at least 80 or 90 per cent men. They all tend to stick together, too. When I walk into a room, I always make an effort to look confident. My goal is to find the man who looks the strongest character there. If you win them over, then you win the room.

Christy Foster, Founder, Online4Baby

A lot of women shy away from walking into a room on their own. Once you've done it a few times, though, it gets easier. You start to recognize one or two faces and you can go to speak with them. You will meet other people like you and get help, advice and pointers towards building the network you need. They'll have pointers on legal and HR issues. These people are on a similar journey and it is a great way to collectively fast track your learning.

Meeting other entrepreneurs is also quite reassuring. You'll realize they've all made, or are making, the same mistakes as you. They've all got half a plan and half a product. But, they'll have the same passion and energy that you do. That can be inspiring. It'll give entrepreneurs the confidence they need at an early stage.

Zandra Moore, Founder and CEO, Panintelligence

The only way to network well is to throw yourself in at the deep end. It might feel easier to lurk on the sidelines, hoping to spot a familiar face, but it is not going to be productive. Apart from anything, the goal is to meet new contacts. The only way to do this is, as Christy says, to walk into the centre of the room and begin speaking to someone.

Planning ahead will make a big difference to the value derived from an event, as well as calming any pre-game jitters. A quick look at the invite will show what sort of people are likely to be there, or even better there will be a complete guest list. Even if a list of attendees is not offered, ask for one. I always do. Founders can then focus on who they might talk to on the day, to get the information they need. I always plan to touch base with a number of people I already know and then to meet a handful I don't.

If, like many people, you struggle with putting a name to a face, don't worry. After spotting a group of three people talking and recognizing one, I will approach and address that person, saying something like 'Hi, I haven't seen you for a while, how are you?'

All being well, as they speak, their response will give some clues about how you know them. This conversational starter will also open the way to break the ice with the others in the group.

'I don't think we've met,' you can say, turning to look at them.

This is the cue for the original person to make the introductions. (Hopefully, they won't struggle with placing the names and faces quite so much.)

Other conversation openers include 'Have you been nominated for a prize?' (at an awards ceremony); or 'This place is filling up quickly, isn't it?

Do you know anybody?' (if they say yes, ask them to introduce you to them).

Asking questions encourages other people to talk, and all you need to do is listen carefully and take advantage of any openings.

I always advise female entrepreneurs to be very careful about the language they use. In particular, I believe we should apologise less. In fact, let's not apologise at all. Don't kick off a conversation with 'I'm sorry to interrupt.' Find a gap in the flow and say something incisive. Similarly, no female entrepreneur should constantly feel they need to explain their credentials (in full) before they say what they have to say. There is no need for founders to justify themselves by going through their entire career and professional qualifications to date. Starting a new business is all the credibility they need.

Remember, too, that networking is a two-way street. Others are there to find out something, too. For this reason, I always do a lot of general prep for these events. In fact, I've always prided myself on being the one in the room who knows most about a particular subject. In some cases, I'd learned it all the previous evening! The point is, though, I can add value for everyone and this opens doors and makes contacts. Finally, as part of the preparation, it is advisable to make sure that your elevator pitch is up-to-date. This is how you introduce both yourself and your business idea in a clear and concise way.

Anyone who fears networking events, and entrepreneurs of both genders do, needs to accept that there will always be some sort of inner battle inside their heads in the run-up to each one. It is impossible to entirely get rid of these self-doubts, but it does get easier over time and with repetition. Here is the thing, though: the more you say your personal and business elevator pitch, the more you will believe it yourself. The more believable you become, the harder it is for people to dismiss what you have to say. Not every event will be a resounding success. Perseverance wins the day, though.

> Nine out of ten networking events will be absolutely dire and I feel like I'd rather have put bolts in my eyes than been there. Then, there will be one chance conversation somewhere that joins the dots and helps me do something I would not have been able to do otherwise.
>
> **Alex Depledge, Founder and CEO, Resi**

As time goes on and the business begins to scale, it is easy to assume that there will be less requirement to network. In truth, though, there will always be a need to get out and make contacts. The demands of the business and senior team will change at each level, meaning there is a constant need for new skills and support. The types of events may change, but entrepreneurs should be prepared to spend a lot of time getting to know new people as their enterprise works towards unicorn status. It's particularly inspiring talking to other entrepreneurs who have already completed the journey.

Building and scaling your own business can be quite a lonely game. The more you get to meet other people who have built high-growth businesses, the more you can embrace the mindset. One of the biggest barriers to high growth is getting into the mindset of what it is like to run a really large organization. Start-ups get to their first million in revenue and it just seems such a challenge to get to the next stage. Founders think: I'm just going to stay at a million – it's too hard to take it further. Other people who have already made it will give you the confidence to be big. Entrepreneurs who have built businesses that have scaled can show that it is possible to get to £5 million, then onto £20 million. If anyone is willing to share all the stages of the journey, it is well worth listening to them.

Sam Smith, Founder, finnCap

Mentors

One possible way to sidestep at least some networking obligations is to work with a mentor. A well-connected mentor can introduce female founders to contacts in their own circle of investors, partners or clients, opening doors that might otherwise have remained closed. Or so the thinking goes.

While much has been written about how mentoring is the key to unlocking the potential of female entrepreneurs and helping to level the playing field, I believe it is very much a matter of personal taste. While mentors can indeed give their protégés access to their contacts, as well as valuable insights on everything from leading a business to marketing and, of course, a much-needed confidence boost, it is something that needs careful thought. Working with the wrong mentor can even be counterproductive. I certainly wouldn't think of it as an easy trade-off to kill any need to network.

Over the years, many people have tried to mentor me, but what has put me off is that they tend to encourage female entrepreneurs to *moderate* their behaviour, while they tell the male equivalent to *stretch* their ambitions. Countless would-be mentors advised me against the idea of starting a bank. Later, once Starling Bank was established, I was strongly warned not to write a book about my experiences founding a company. The implications were clear: Why did *I* think I should write a book? And, it is not very *polite*, is it? In both cases (albeit with the benefit of hindsight) I can say with great conviction that my potential advisors were wrong. The bank I started became successful and profitable. Meanwhile, *Banking On It*, the bestselling book about how I did it, became a crucial tool in growing the business.[3] When new investors wanted to know about Starling Bank, we could send them a copy, which told them everything they needed to know about our background, culture and values. The same went for new employees.

Since the business has been established, I've met all sorts of people who have told me they would have been helpful and supportive if I had met them earlier. Privately, I wonder if they would have been. The problem with my idea was it didn't particularly fit into a neat box. I was starting a bank and most people didn't really get it because, at the time, no one just started a bank (as I was told, numerous times). I have spoken with other successful entrepreneurs and heard a similar story. Their idea was successful because they did something completely different, but they struggled to get it off the ground or find the mentoring support they needed for the exact same reason. It's frustrating to say it, but support mechanisms are largely geared towards businesses that look like other businesses.

Something else that I am wary of is that there are people who will use the mentorship label to try to muscle their way in, if they can see a new founder might be on to something. This was the experience of Zandra Moore.

I met a man at a networking event and was a bit surprised when he turned up at the office unannounced and asked for a meeting. Within five minutes of getting in front of me he said: 'I'm here to tell you that you need me and your business will fail without me.'

'Why is that?' I asked, a little bemused.

'You've got no older people,' he said.

Bearing in mind I was 36 years old at the time and he was only around 10 years older than me, it seemed a bit ridiculous. His pitch seemed to be that there were no senior people and we needed people (like him) with experience to make sure everyone was doing their jobs right. More specifically, a man like him. I had to tell him that we really, really didn't need his services.

> Sadly, this is not an uncommon experience. A lot of people have told me I am going to fail without someone senior in my business. People pitch themselves to be that person because they can see the opportunity, but there isn't one. One guy sent me a pretty unpleasant, aggressive email, telling me I would regret it.
>
> **Zandra Moore, Founder and CEO, Panintelligence**

Taking all this into account, it should also be said that there are many successful female founders who swear by the effectiveness of mentoring. Female mentors in particular can be hugely helpful when it comes to helping their protégés navigate the challenges specific to female entrepreneurs. There is also a lot of value to be had from regularly changing mentors as an entrepreneur progresses through their high-growth journey, because successive mentors can be right for different stages. In this latter case, not all mentors need to be female. Male mentors with specific skill sets can be invaluable too. I've been told that it can also work quite well to have mentors at a similar stage, the idea being that you can co-mentor each other, because it is inevitable you will go through different experiences. I'm not sure I entirely agree on this last point. A different name for this level of mentor would be 'friend'.

As with networking, the key to finding the right mentors is preparation. Entrepreneurs should take the time to determine want they want to get out of the relationship, which will help with choosing the right person to work with. It will also help in creating a plan of action once a relationship is established.

Connecting with a mentor is a lot easier when there's already a link. It's simply a case of a polite request and, all being well, an answer in the affirmative. Failing that, entrepreneurs will need to do the equivalent of cold calling potential mentors to ask if they'll consider giving up some of their time. This can either be done through networking events, as above, or via emails.

When I started out, I had no qualms about calling someone I had never met before and asking for half an hour of their time. Some people said yes, but the majority said no, or ignored me altogether. I'm on the other side of that process now and receive hundreds of emails asking me for half an hour of my time. I clearly can't see everyone, as I have too much else going on. So, if you wanted some time from an established entrepreneur like me, how would you break through? My advice is to make yourself *interesting*. Think about what you'd like to see in an email establishing contact that would make you think: this person sounds like someone I'd like to meet.

Persistence is key here, too. There is little point in emailing a potential mentor and then, after receiving no response, becoming consumed with self-doubt and never trying again. Follow up with another email. You can even use the exact same one again. We are far too quick to make assumptions. We see things through our own lens, where we are naturally the centre of our own universe. If we send a message to someone and get no response, we decide that the recipient wasn't interested, or thinks we are not worth replying to. In reality, there could be a multitude of reasons for the silence and high up in this list is the recipient didn't really register the email because they had other things going on when it landed. Just remember this: if they didn't respond the first time, it is highly likely that they won't remember the original message. If, by any chance, they do respond the second time to say 'Haven't you already sent me this email?' then that's great. 'Well, yes I have,' could be the reply. 'And thank you so much for responding this time. I am just so keen to get your input on…'

It's a breakthrough if anyone does agree to be a mentor, particularly if it is an industry figure you greatly admire. However, the relationship will get rocky if the onus is on the mentor to maintain it. Mentees should keep in regular touch, to take away some of that burden. Successful entrepreneurs are busy people, so they are highly unlikely to be free for daily phone calls. They are more likely to respond to text messages, emails or voicemail with specific questions or requests, which they can answer in their own time-frame. Even if a few messages go by without an answer, mentees should make the effort to keep their mentor up-to-date with progress. If they've agreed to the relationship, they'll most likely to respond when they get a window.

Being a successful entrepreneur takes more than simply a good idea, the right expertise and commitment. It pays to have someone in your corner, whether it is providing advice or much-needed support. In every case, though, finding the *right* source of help can make all the difference.

Notes

[1] I Woodford. The UK's most active accelerators, ranked, Sifted, 17 January 2022. sifted.eu/articles/uk-accelerators-tech-nation-upscale (archived at https://perma.cc/DW9S-AGLQ)

[2] The Up Group. www.theupgroup.com (archived at https://perma.cc/JT8H-B9PP)

[3] A Boden (2021) *Banking On It: How I disrupted an industry and changed the way we manage our money forever*, Penguin Business, London

CHAPTER FOUR

Co-founders

Business is a numbers game, or so the saying goes. The numbers here almost always refer to the balance sheet or the profit and loss. Yet, well before a founder gets to the stage of balancing the books, there is a very important numerical decision they need to make: how many people will lead the business?

The person who first came up with a business idea might like the idea of going solo. This would give them the control and freedom to run the company themselves. At the same time though, setting up and scaling a high-growth business is a daunting endeavour, requiring a multitude of skill sets. When it comes to tackling the challenges ahead, two heads, or three, or even four, could be better than one.

There are pros and cons to both. The stats show that 80 per cent of unicorns have two or three co-founders, but turn that on its head and that still means a respectable 20 per cent of billion pound plus enterprises were led by a solo founder.[1] In that number are Amazon, Dell, eBay and Tumblr. Among female-founded businesses, aside from myself, solo founders who reached unicorn status in the past few years include Nicole Sahin who is behind Globalization Partners, the employer record company, Deepika Bodapati who founded health monitoring giant Athelas, and Rachel Drori of frozen food delivery service Daily Harvest.

It can be a question of timing. If, say, a small group of uni mates got together and came up with an idea and were fully and equally involved from the beginning of a project, then they would rightly be seen as, and share the title of, co-founder. Where things are not so clear cut is where a single entrepreneur comes up with an idea and then opts to bring in additional senior people to fill in gaps in their skill set. In this case, it is possible that the person who created the start-up would go by the title 'founder' but the new partners would take a slightly lower status and become known as co-founders. Alternatively, the original founder may wish to present the business to the outside world as a fully co-founded one.

I was always destined to be a sole founder, but was more than willing to give out co-founder titles. In fact, in the first year I gave them out like they were sweets. In start-ups, co-founder can also be a euphemism for not being paid. It's one of the few weapons that an entrepreneur has in their armoury. When they are not able to pay people, the next best thing they can do is to offer a good title, a badge. If someone can be persuaded to believe in your vision, they will welcome the opportunity. *If this business does as well as she says it will, I will be a successful co-founder.*

As a caveat, it is prudent to think about how such titles can look at a later date, should the business take off and the co-founder remain. We gave one colleague the title of 'co-founder and troubleshooter', a title he proudly signed off any communication with for some time. It was only once we were established and sending documents to banking regulators that we realized we needed to make sure it didn't get included on certain outside communications. It didn't quite have the gravitas required by the authorities. Nevertheless, he was the most diligent person on the planet and was actually the troubleshooter that I relied upon for a wide range of actions.

I have also made mistakes in the past, awarding titles because at the time I needed to tell the world that we had breadth of talent. Most people in this situation understand that the influence that they have in the organization doesn't measure up to the title and frequently decide to rapidly move on to monetize the situation in another job elsewhere.

Even with the great title, it doesn't mean founders can take advantage of people; they need to make sure everyone is happy and involved. Plus, when in a position to pay, pay them well. It is also important for a founder to be humble. Stand for a free lunch for everyone on a Friday or arrange for a round of coffees to be brought in. (Don't bring the coffees in yourself. As a woman, it is unwise to be seen doing something this domesticated.) These things all make a big difference. The goal is to influence people and engage them in the start-up and the task ahead. The team is a founder's greatest asset and you need to do everything in your power to retain them and also to make sure they benefit from all the upside.

Ultimately, the decision behind whether an entrepreneur presents themselves as a solo or co-founder will have implications all the way down the line, so it is good to be armed with the facts from the start. Some of the key considerations here are expertise, funding, friction and the level of support that might be needed. Let's look at each one in more detail.

Expertise

Entrepreneurs need to be able to turn their hands to almost everything and most of us are pretty good at this. But, are we *brilliant* at everything? Probably not. And in a high-growth business we do need to cover all the bases. It's not just that, though. The other question to ask is, do you *enjoy* doing everything?

Those who believe strongly in the benefits of a co-founder partnership invariably argue that the greatest benefit is that the people involved will have strengths and ideas that complement and build upon those of the other founders. The scope of these strengths cover everything from intellectual to creative skills, to how each person interacts with others. Founders who know themselves to be an introvert, for example, might like to bring in an extrovert co-founder to deal with the outward-facing stuff that would normally fill them with dread. In an ideal world, each founder would be a bit of both, introvert and extrovert, thus fully equipped to focus on the strategic side but also able to jump in and get their hands a little dirty too. We don't, however, live in a perfect world.

> I am very lucky with Jules, my co-founder. We came from very similar backgrounds, but are very different in every way. She is quite geeky and quiet, whereas I am a loud extrovert. We were thrown together on a project when she was 20 and I was 25, and just got on straight away. We had the same values and complementary skill sets. Since she is very techy, she takes the chief technology officer role and I take the people-facing stuff.
>
> **Alex Depledge, Founder and CEO, Resi**

There is a counter-argument. Say one person has a great idea, but feels communications is not their strength and cedes part of the business to a more sales orientated co-founder. Joanna Jensen, the solo founder behind Childs Farm, the UK's number one baby and child toiletries brand, says this can be a mistake. She believes that the person who has the initial idea is by far the best placed to sell it, whatever their perceived weaknesses.

> There are a lot of brilliantly talented founders who just believe they don't have the ability to articulate the key selling points of their idea. They follow the school of thought that says if you don't have the confidence to do it yourself, you should bring in a co-founder to do the talking. I believe the true passion and sparkle in the eyes that convinces others to believe is most dominant in the person who came up with the original idea. A committed founder feels so strongly about their business that it becomes an extension of themselves, and that passion will always come across. You should be able to rely on capable and committed members of your leadership team – such as a strong commercial director – to articulate your vision and the brand in their areas of expertise; it doesn't have to be a co-founder. A founder who doesn't feel they have the confidence to present can also seek professional help through coaching, which can make a huge difference.
>
> **Joanna Jensen, Founder, Childs Farm**

Funding: Investors and solo founders

While VCs do fund solo founders, some investors are adamant that single founders are almost impossible to back. This was the experience of June Angelides when she sought out angel funding for her venture Mums In Tech, which offered child-friendly coding schools for mums. She found she couldn't access these sources of capital because she pitched as a solo founder and funds ruled that there needed to be a co-founder in order to process any application. June is now an investor herself at Samos Investments and, partly thanks to her experience, focuses on female founders.

> Even though more investors are funding solo founders, and I do so myself, I do see that, in these situations, investors are still always looking for the holes. They want to know where a solo founder may not have the strengths necessary to see the business plan through. This is essentially what co-founders do: complement each other's strengths and weaknesses.
>
> **June Angelides, Investor, Samos Investments**

What is important to note here is: this stance is very much led by investors. There is nothing that says a single founder is less effective than a pair, or more than one co-founder. Investors insist on more than one founder for a single reason – to protect their investment. The train of thought goes that if anything happened to one party, the other co-founder/s would be able to step up, keep things going and realize everything that was promised on the business plan. Likewise, if a founder leaves, the remaining team would not find themselves in a position where the majority of stock is held by someone no longer in the business.

No investor ever says this bit out loud, because it would look like they didn't trust a founder. Instead, it is more commonly couched in terms of the value of shared expertise, as above: i.e. there needs to be more than one founder because it will increase the range of skills on offer. Everyone on the senior team will be able to bring different, complementary qualities.

What investors are not as eager to acknowledge is that there are also challenges with multiple founders. If everyone has ostensibly equal status, then everyone wants to be in charge and this can lead to petty and time-consuming infighting. The partnership can even fall apart at the seams as a result. Eventually, one founder will come out on top who may or may not have been the person who initially came up with the idea and brought the founding team together. What is most galling is it is often the *investors* who get the final say on who is in or out. They will choose the most likely boss.

Friction

Running a business, and in particular a high-growth one, will put more pressure on your relationships with those alongside you than anything you could ever imagine. The friction between me and my co-founder Tom Blomfield, who went on to launch Starling Bank rival Monzo, has been well documented. When Tom walked out, taking my entire team with him during a challenging funding round, it was the closest the digital bank came to failing. I called it Starling's 'near-death' experience and it was one of the most stressful times of my life. I faced the prospect of starting all over again, with zero likelihood of any sort of investment in the foreseeable future.

Anyone who has been around entrepreneurs for any time will be able to tell you some horror stories about co-founder break-ups. They happen for a multitude of reasons. Perhaps the communication between the team is not what it should have been and everyone has a slightly different picture of the end goal. This inevitably leads to frustrations spilling over, when a business comes up against one of the many crossroads it will inevitably hit on its journey to scale. The original founder may also discover that their carefully chosen co-founders are not quite as capable of withstanding the pressure of running a high-growth enterprise. Alternatively, if the skill sets of two co-founders are too close there will be the slightly awkward and less-than-optimal situation where they both fulfil similar roles, yet try to differentiate between themselves by giving themselves titles like chief executive officer and chief operations officer. Unless the COO is focused on purely operations, there is no need for two such senior roles in a start-up, certainly not with such focus on business strategy. One of the biggest reasons why relations break down is when levels of commitment are mismatched. Start-up life is a 24/7 endeavour. If a founder gives a co-founder a great title and a number of shares, and discovers he or she is working the bare minimum, then frustrations will always erupt. It is impossible to remove the title, or take away the shares, so there is only really one option: to part company with the co-founder. If you want to know why real co-founders stay the course, it's because they are fully committed to the plan.

There can be no guarantees that the co-founding team will always work together smoothly, particularly when the pressure is on. Disagreement, stress and conflict are part and parcel of the start-up story. However, it is possible to take precautions when putting together the top team. It is crucial they have something in common and a similar set of values. Each one may be different ages and from diverse backgrounds, but their principles will be complementary. At Starling, for example, the top team we subsequently put together was very cerebral and risk adverse – unusual for a start-up but great for a bank start-up where looking after people's money is a huge responsibility. The nature of the business means we needed to be like this. Other start-ups might seek out co-founders who want to shock the marketplace. What is most important is there needs to be a fundamental approach you all agree on.

Plus, of course, a key consideration which can't ever be dismissed is whether you actually *like* your co-founders. It is inevitable that you will be spending a lot of time together. Can you see yourself building a close relationship?

Support

There is another side to the friction point mentioned above. A co-founder will be the only other person on the planet who truly understands the stresses and strains that their business partners are going through. They will live the same intense highs and lows and be on the exact same page, which means they can be a vital source of support at the toughest times.

> When I am down, Jules picks me up and vice versa – when she is down, I pick her up. We are in a high-pressured game and it is easy to come apart at the seams.
>
> **Alex Depledge, Founder and CEO, Resi**

Support is, however, not a strong enough reason on its own to bring in a co-founder. Co-founders will expect equity and the question any founder needs to ask themselves is this: how much of their business are they prepared to give away for this level of support? It would be better to elicit the same level of support by creating and engaging a team that is fully behind the objective.

How to find and sign up a co-founder

As any founder will attest, finding the perfect co-founder is tough. The first big task is identifying the right person for the job, which isn't always as straightforward as it sounds. Something I have come across a few times is where candidates appear well suited to take up the role of high-growth business co-founder, but turn out to be entirely inappropriate. Despite seeming to tick the right boxes on paper, closer scrutiny will reveal they don't actually have the same level of experience they may boast about. It's a lot more common than you might think. In fact, try this exercise yourself; do a quick search on LinkedIn for people who claim to be a founder of a successful start-up. There will be dozens connected with a single start-up. Now, it is quite possible they had a role to play in the early days. That role may even have been vitally important when the company was small. But, the implication of their post is that they took the start-up through from the early days to becoming a household name. Trading for ever more on their position as 'co-founder' of a major organization may be over-egging it a little.

In the earliest days of my own start-up journey, I met a number of people like this. They looked brilliant on paper and then, when they began working with me, it all fell apart. They'd speak in jargon because they seemed to think that was how people spoke at start-ups, or make bizarre and costly decisions more suited to corporates, perhaps because that was really their main background. In one example, a co-founder kept disappearing at odd times. One day, he called up and said he'd been fired. We were all a little confused by this because, despite his somewhat erratic behaviour, we had not dismissed him. It transpired that he was still working for another firm, in parallel, while spending most of his time with Starling. He'd been merely pretending he was doing his first job. It was very odd. He'd been very excited about being part of a start-up, but had, you might say, failed to fully commit. It would be good to say this was my only bad experience, but it wasn't. Another potential co-founder, who talked up his coding skills, was found to be using a software house in India to do his work.

As well as carefully checking credentials, there is a job to be done ensuring a potential co-founder has complementary strengths and weaknesses, balancing out the things that you're good at and not so adept at. If the candidate under scrutiny has too many similar skills, there's not much point bringing them in.

Some entrepreneurs consider signing up either a trusted friend, or even a member of their own family. The thinking goes that this is playing it safe because they know this person well already. Plus, the existing, possibly long-term, link is a sign that everyone gets along.

As a rule, it is best to steer away from filling a start-up with close friends and family, particularly in a co-founder's role. For any business to scale, it needs the optimum team from the start, with evidence of expertise in their particular area. The tendency here is to squeeze family or friends into filling a particular position, even when it might not be in their skill set, or meet the brief of shoring up a founder's weakness. Then, there is the ever-present possibility that a high-growth business won't make it. If this happens, more than the company will be lost. There will be a real possibility of a long-term family rift, or the loss of a close friend.

Online4Baby founder Christy Foster is the rare exception to this rule. When her business began growing, she encouraged her husband to give up his job as site manager for a large electricity company to join her firm. She also brought in her sister and brother-in-law.

> They all had good jobs before, but I persuaded them to come in with me, telling them they could double or triple what they earned. The business was quite small at the time and their bosses thought they were mad.
>
> It works because we are all different, bring different skills and opinions and all work in very diverse roles. We are also careful not to talk about work outside of work.
>
> **Christy Foster, Founder, Online4Baby**

As Christy has shown, this arrangement can work, but it is a risk, especially during the early days of an, as yet, unproven venture. At this stage, the start-up is facing enough jeopardy, so founders are best advised look outside their inner circle for co-founders.

Loose connections gained from previous roles are often a useful starting point. These contacts will not necessarily be close friends, but they know you well enough to be willing to start a conversation. Similarly, thanks to that earlier connection, you already have at least a vague idea of their background, as well as their strengths and weaknesses. Your networking efforts may also come into their own here, too. Don't be afraid to ask for recommendations.

If anyone does show an interest, this will mark the first big selling job (in a long line) for a founder and their company. It is an acid test to convince a potential co-founder to buy into the idea, drop whatever it is they are doing – and the secure wage they are receiving – to throw in their lot with a start-up which may or may not succeed. To do this, an entrepreneur will need to go all-out to talk up the brilliant prospects of the business and convince the other party that they are going to reap the rewards of this exciting journey.

Should an entrepreneur succeed in setting up a meeting with a potential co-founder, there are two essential pieces of advice to follow. The first is not to arrive brandishing a non-disclosure agreement (NDA) which you demand is signed before you utter a word because you don't want to give anything away of your idea without one. There is nothing that is more designed to stop the Big Sell in its tracks. I never, ever sign an NDA before agreeing to a meeting. It just doesn't make sense. Say, for example, I have been thinking about launching the Big Purple Bank and then signed an NDA with an unknown start-up. When we meet, that same start-up may breathlessly extol the virtues of the business they are planning, based on the idea of a Big Purple Bank. This would leave me in a terrible situation. Realistically, I should be able to start my own business, based on my earlier idea, but this would tie my hands entirely.

> You are at the stage of 1 per cent idea and 1 per cent product right now. That is all you have. Your business is your energy and your ability to execute. You don't need an NDA for that. Get your idea out there. No one is going to pinch it. Even if they tried to, they won't have the passion, commitment and energy to make it succeed without you.
>
> **Zandra Moore, Founder and CEO, Panintelligence**

Once someone has bought into the idea, you can then introduce a basic NDA, along with the rest of the co-founder legal agreements, covering employment terms, undertakings and shareholdings.

The second point to avoid is making an even a casual mention about how long the journey might be. There is an expectation that with some hard work and maybe a little luck, a good idea will see exponential growth quite quickly. Nothing ever happens as fast as you'd expect it to, especially with high-growth businesses. If that was vocalized, though, it would be very difficult to persuade anyone to join.

Shares and the small print

And, so to the first potential source of conflict between co-founders: the allocation of equity. If there are two founders, do they split the available shares down the middle, 50:50? Or, does the founder that came up with the idea get a greater share? According to Y Combinator founder Paul Graham, unequal divisions of equity resulted in founders leaving around 20 per cent of the accelerator's start-ups.[2] Assigning a low percentage share is taken as a sign that the co-founder is not valued and, in the long term, this will be counterproductive.

> There is nothing worse than the partner who has the original idea taking a 60 per cent stake, while giving their co-founder 40 per cent. Seven or ten years down the line, that original idea will mean nothing if the business is successful. It is all in the execution. Yet, to the co-founder who has the 40 per cent, that 20 per cent less will mean everything. You have to go into this with trust in each

other and complete fairness. If there in inequality at the start, it will stir up trouble for years to come. Make sure it is a fair split, a 50:50 partnership.

Alex Depledge, Founder and CEO, Resi

There are drawbacks to equal splits. One partner might overvalue past contributions, whether it is coming up with the idea, or building a prototype, and then undervalue their future contribution, or become less committed. Again, this can cause conflict and bitterness.

Another potential flash point arises when there are three founders involved and shares are distributed on an equal basis. If there is a dispute, two founders could use their combined equity stake to vote the third one out.

My own viewpoint is that assigning equity can be a point of vulnerability for female founders. If there is an imbalance and there are more male co-founders than female ones, they can get together to force a woman out. This can, and does, happen if a company looks like it is about to be successful. The female founder's equity will then be distributed to those who remain. One (unusual) way to avoid this is for a female founder not to vest their equity while all the co-founders that subsequently join the team always vest. Vesting is the process where founders become entitled to their shares over time – if they leave then they lose the unvested shares. If the female founder does not vest, their shares are theirs to keep and there is less chance of them being eased out of the company. I did this and it did give me some protection. I am duty bound to add that investors were not keen on the arrangement. In retrospect, this could be why it took me two years to raise money. What I did was extremely unusual and it did frequently come up in discussions with investors.

This is a good moment to remind founders that the agreement with co-founders will be very carefully scrutinized by investors when the time comes. Thus, as well as coming to an agreement as to who owns how much equity, there needs to be a written record. At this stage, though, there is no need to spend a fortune on lawyers, particularly since there will be zero money in the business. In the worst-case scenario, a founder will agree that each of their co-founders will get an equal share, and will spend a few weeks getting bogged down in the legal side, only for one of the founders to drop out well before the investment round. All that time and money will have been wasted. Get a basic agreement signed and further firm it up just ahead of the investment round. It is inevitable that a huge amount will have changed between this time and starting to pitch for money. Focus your efforts on getting the business to that stage. If too much time is spent on discussing who will get what, nothing will ever get built.

Do, though, make sure any agreement is formalized. All being well, the start-up will grow quickly and take on a life of its own. But if something goes wrong along the way it'll make things a lot easier during the inevitable fall-out.

Notes

[1]   A Tamaseb. Land of the 'super founders': A data-driven approach to uncover the secrets of billion dollar startups, Medium, 5 December 2018. alitamaseb.medium.com/land-of-the-super-founders-a-data-driven-approach-to-uncover-the-secrets-of-billion-dollar-a69ebe3f0f45 (archived at https://perma.cc/D52N-JCG5)

[2]   Harvard University Office of Technology Development. Startup Guide: An entrepreneur's guide for Harvard University faculty, graduate students, and postdoctoral fellows, Harvard University, 2011. otd.harvard.edu/uploads/Files/OTD_Startup_Guide.pdf (archived at https://perma.cc/8UX4-W6LV)

CHAPTER FIVE

Building a strong start-up team

Watch any film or TV portrayal of start-up life, it is always very pally. There will be a sizeable group of young people, hailing from largely the same backgrounds, who seem to find time for a lot of banter as they sit astride soft chairs, or lounge on colourful cushions in stylish, glass-walled break-out rooms. The reality is very different.

The goal of any start-up should be to hire as few people as possible, and as for the fancy office, forget it. Early iterations of Starling Bank went through three offices in as many years because the number one criteria was the cheapest space possible. We scooped up super-short leases from landlords who were about to sell up, or refurbish or, in one case, where the building was about to be knocked down altogether to make way for a redevelopment. They were keen to squeeze out the last few months of rental, and it meant we got space in central London at a knock down price.

Why do start-ups make the mistake of over-hiring and paying over the odds for an office? Perhaps because it *feels* like the first step on the way to becoming a 'proper business'. When founders talk about what they are up to, one of the first questions they'll be asked is: 'How many employees do you have?' A large number has somehow become a metric for success, or to show how cool this start-up is. The tendency to over-hire is particularly prevalent among those who previously had a corporate career. Anyone who was once in a management position can find it hard to shake the comfort blanket of being surrounded by a team of people they can marshal.

Hiring too many people is a classic way to burn through cash – fast. When the team numbers tick up, it leads to a high burn rate, which means a start-up begins to lose a huge amount of money each month. It's completely unsustainable, adding more pressure onto an already highly pressurized situation. Founders need to turn the 'how many employees' question on its head, and boast about *how much* they are getting done with *so few* people. Yes, they will end up doing things that others used to do for them, but that is part and parcel of the start-up package.

The first people to hire

For a tech-based high-growth business, the priority will be to bring in people who can code and who can go out and get users. It may well be that the founder and/or their co-founders fulfil one or both of these roles. It might help to outline here the positions that need to be filled very early on. The list may, of course, vary depending upon the specific needs of the start-up, but anticipate a need for some or all the following:

- **Chief executive officer (CEO)**
  The CEO controls the big picture, such as the company's direction, vision and culture.

- **Chief operations officer (COO)**
  The COO focuses on the day-to-day operations that keep the start-up running. This is the person who will typically answer a customer query at 2am when all the other staff have gone home!

- **Chief technology officer (CTO)**
  This role is crucial to the success of any high-growth business, since technology is almost always the key to scaling. In fact, if you are a tech start-up, you won't be taken seriously unless an engineer co-founder is part of the core team. While the start-up may well rely on freelance engineers to begin with, there needs to be someone who fully understands this side of the operation to keep things moving in the right direction.

- **Product manager**
  Product managers manage the product strategy, vision and development, working closely with the engineering and marketing team. At the very beginning, this will be down to the founder, but employing an expert can be a wise investment.

- **Chief marketing officer (CMO)**
  High-growth businesses need customers, a lot of them in almost every case, so this role will be invaluable. CMOs focus on customers and how they view the product or service. They will also interact with the product manager to incorporate customer feedback into product development.

- **Chief financial officer (CFO)**
  There is a school of thought that the tasks undertaken by a CFO can be outsourced in the early days. However, since the financial health of a start-up is so crucial for its future prospects, there's value in prioritizing this role which manages all aspects of the company finances, ranging from early loans, to property and equipment leases, to paying suppliers and managing the petty cash.

My grandmother was an entrepreneur, running hugely successful hotel and then antiques businesses. She instilled in me a number of lessons, chief among them the importance of turnover, turnover, turnover. She told me never to tie up all my cash in stock, because then you will have no cash to invest in marketing. So many businesses go bust because they don't allow for this.

I invested in one start-up and was shocked to see, post-fund raise, that they seem to put their feet up for a few months. They thought they were fine because they had just got a chunk of money in the bank. Cash management is a constant task. You have to balance cash in stock vs distribution certainty vs marketing opportunities vs paying your staff. If you don't manage your cash, you are more likely to fail.

Joanna Jensen, Founder, Childs Farm

- **Customer service representative**
  It is impossible for a business to survive, let alone scale, if it doesn't look after its customers, and even more so in today's highly connected world where no one is afraid to call out a bad experience. A customer service representative protects the brand by building positive relationships with customers.

- **Sales manager**
  This person will focus on generating leads and bringing in revenue for a B2B start-up. Their success, or otherwise, is key to the speed of growth.

- **Business development manager**
  Similar to the above, the job of the business development manager is to grow a B2B business, but in this case from a marketing and sales point of view. They will identify opportunities from both within the organization, and outside, either in the existing target market or in new markets entirely.

> If you want to scale quickly, you need people who know what 'good' looks like. Otherwise, you run the risk of reinventing HR, finance, operations and fulfilment, but not necessarily in a productive way. It's that analogy of driving a car at 100 miles per hour, while changing all the parts. People forget about the 'changing the parts' bit and the organizational transformation that needs to keep it all happening to keep it all going. If it doesn't happen, it will fall apart.
>
> **Tania Boler, Founder, Elvie**

Something to add to Tania's point is, don't hire people for roles too many stages ahead. My first dedicated HR person was laser-focused on building a HR system for a company employing 60,000 people when our numbers were still in the low hundreds.

The digital economy has spawned an entire ecosystem of companies servicing the start-up world, whether it is payments systems or payroll. Buy in the correct functions for the size of company you are now, or will be in the immediate future, and scale them as you go along. The energies of the company, and finances, need to go into elements that will generate products or customers. Don't become too fixated on spending too much time on working on supporting functions. In a funding round, investors care about the service your company is delivering to customers and not whether the business has a fantastic internal staff newsletter.

While the descriptions of each role in a start-up sound very exact, the start-up reality is there will be some crossover in the very early days. If the marketing hire is a wordsmith, they will be worth their weight in gold for writing documents, from detailing technical processes to liquidity management. Likewise, the COO may initially extend their operations role to look after some aspects of the finances, such as managing invoicing, funding allocation and approval of expenditure. Ideally, the CTO will share some of the product management brief, by spotting gaps in the market that could potentially lead to the development of the next big product. Everyone's core skills will be stretched to the limit.

What is on offer?

Setting out to hire a team when there is little more in place than a great idea can be a daunting prospect. The goal is to bring in the brightest and the best, but they need to be convinced of the opportunity when there is nothing of real note to show off yet. Just to put the pressure on, there is a war for talent out there, particularly for certain tech-based roles.

To be clear here, there is no need to pay *over* the market rate to secure the best tech talent, although you must pay the going rate. However, with a limited pool of top talent, founders have to differentiate themselves from other potential employers. The way to succeed in this is to make the job seem engaging, compelling and, well, irresistible; all of which requires a big sales job. In Starling's case, we needed to convince our tech hires that what was on offer was going to be so much more interesting than working with high-street banks. Equally importantly, anyone on our tech team would have an opportunity to change things. Really change things. Tech teams working for large organizations rarely get to properly see the fruits of their labour. It can take months, even years, for even small changes to take effect. With a business such as Starling, anything innovative might be out on the app within days because the feedback loop is designed for a fast response and to get updates to market quickly. We were (and still are) an engineer-friendly organization and recognize that engineers are the most critical hires we make.

What this all means is, to win the war for talent, you need to be very clear about the vision and the path to growth, finding a succinct, compelling way to share the USP of the start-up with potential hires and setting out exactly what you expect, as well as the career opportunity on offer.

Thought should be given to *where* everyone will work, because this will have a bearing on the attractiveness of the role. Does every member of the team need to be in the office every day? A lot of people have embraced the benefits of home working since the pandemic and I am one of them. Before the global health crisis, I was the type who was always in the office. I'd usually be the first in and often the last out. I now feel a very different way and suspect that I will probably never return to my old ways. Like most entrepreneurs, I'm very happy to continue to work most waking hours, weekends as well as weekdays, but accept that I don't have to be in the office all the time to be effective.

I do wonder if the same applies to a start-up. It might seem instinctive to err on the side of flexibility, where some people can opt to work from the office, some from home and others a hybrid of the two, because this may seem an important metric when it comes to people deciding whether or not to join. However, a start-up feels like a unique situation. I'm not sure that there will be the required sense of momentum and urgency if everyone is in a different location. Plus, in a situation where no one is being paid, what is to stop them moonlighting for a handful of start-ups as they hedge their bets to see which one breaks away and shows promise? Then, there is the possibility that if everyone is given free rein to make a choice, it could unwittingly create a situation where home workers become second class citizens compared to those who are 'present and correct' in the office each day.

All team members need to see that there's potential for them on a personal level. One of the big reasons that people eschew 'safe' jobs in the corporate world is that by joining a start-up there is a lot more chance of taking a big leap forward and accelerating their career. Entrepreneurial ventures offer more responsibility and a wider range of learning opportunities. And, with a smaller team, there is more likelihood that the efforts of each individual will get noticed and any creative suggestions valued. There is also the prospect to grow with the company and take on more challenging roles.

> It's motivating for people who join to see that there are opportunities to progress and we've invested a lot into filling roles internally. Many of the people who used to serve customers, in what we call our beekeeping functions, have moved on into new roles as the company expanded. Our senior customer research manager started off like this, and we've had a fair number of technical transitions too.
>
> **Romi Savova, Founder and CEO, PensionBee**

How to hire well

> I see too many entrepreneurs that are great at what they do, but absolutely hopeless at running the team behind them. They try to run at a million miles an hour and don't realize they need to stop and find a number two, or a number three. This will always limit the size of the business.
>
> You've got to put the time into recruitment and to work out what sort of skills you need around you. You don't need a bunch of mini-mes, either – you need people with the opposite skills to those you're good at.
>
> One of my investments on the *Dragons' Den* TV show was a young lad who was a great front man, a real entrepreneur. But he was not good at managing

things behind the scenes. Generally, if you are good at the outward-facing stuff, you are not so good at the operational bits. His wife came into the business and managed operations. She was the business's salvation.

Jenny Campbell, CEO, YourCash, and former Dragon

Recruitment is always a costly business, but it is possible to cut down on costs and avoid time spent wading through irrelevant CVs by posting very specific job descriptions. Any job outline should also include an accurate and compelling overview of the start-up, its culture, goals and existing team. Careful thought needs to be given to the type of person who would fit into the business. New team members need to be up for the challenge and not afraid to think creatively. Other qualities to look out for might include: self-motivation, leadership skills, ambition, honesty and willingness to work long but fulfilling hours. What is not needed is a recruit with a massive ego. This is the stage in a company's growth where everyone needs to muck in. No one has any time to dance around anyone's ego. As the saying goes: hire for ability, fire for attitude. If a team member doesn't have the right attitude, they will never fit in.

As with co-founders, the search for potential team members should begin with personal contacts and recommendations. Then, depending on the entry level of the position, the job can be posted on platforms like AngelList or LinkedIn, where the search can be optimized at a fraction of the cost of an agency. I spent a lot of time trawling LinkedIn trying to find out where everyone was and what they were doing. When I spoke to people and found they were not interested in Starling, I always asked them to point me in the direction of others they knew who might be a good fit.

This is where female founders outside the capital can be quite fortunate. Leeds, which is where I am from, is like one big village. Most people in my line of business know each other quite well and will almost certainly know someone who would be a good fit. There are never many degrees of separation between a founder looking for someone and a person they'd be able to work quite well with. I don't think that is quite the same in London.

What I have noticed, though, is that men are not keen to go out for a drink with female founders. They think their wife will disapprove. I'm happy to go for a coffee, though. They seem comfortable with that.

Zandra Moore, Founder and CEO, Panintelligence

When it comes to the interview itself, the key is to be as professional as possible to create a powerful first impression, even if the first meeting is going to be in Starbucks. One way to do this is to emulate practices in the corporate sector by starting off with online assessments to measure the candidate's skills and ability and alerting candidates that there may be rounds of interviews scheduled for preferred candidates. Of course, if you are not in a position to pay people at this stage, and are hiring on the basis of 'jam tomorrow', it is not fair to set tests for prospective candidates. Anything that smacks of unfair practice will *always* find its way onto employee search site Glassdoor, and a negative review there is not the sort of profile that any start-up wants.

Before each interview, I always thought hard about how I could sell myself and Starling Bank as an attractive proposition. Something I found very effective was to use 'credibility markers'. One of my earliest successes had been to persuade consultancy firms such as PwC and KPMG to work with us on a contingency basis, whereby I would pay their fees if and when I raised funding. I then made full use of the reputation of my prestigious partners. Never mind that, at the time, my deal with PwC amounted to little more than them allowing me to use their client lounge. Inviting candidates to meet me at PwC's impressive offices spoke volumes and gave me a credibility that otherwise I wouldn't have had as an, as yet, unfunded start-up.

During this interview process, consideration needs to be given to the mix of people who make the final cut. Founders might be tempted to hire people in their own image, because they think they'll all get along well, or bring in a groups with similar personalities because they may gel, but this can be counterproductive.

I made the big error of not looking at how my senior team worked as a whole, and ended up with a really lopsided operation. The top team was very steady. No one wanted to rock the boat and instead they liked to spend time thinking things through. There were a load of storytellers too. This meant there were no analytical people and no drivers. We weren't basing anything on data and no one was driving it forward, apart from me.

I replaced the team. Before I hired a new team, I created a wheel outlining different sorts of personalities. I wasn't just looking for people with the right attitude and who could do the job, they had to take up a role in the leadership team based on their attributes. My head of sales had to be a driver. I didn't need a soft, empathetic person for that job. I didn't need that personality type because I had it elsewhere in the business.

> I ended up with a very well-rounded senior management team that covered all the bases and the whole is greater than the sum of the parts. It's not just the addition, it is a force multiplier. My life became so much better once I figured that out.
>
> **Alex Depledge, Founder and CEO, Resi**

As this story shows, when putting together a start-up team, it is not necessarily a relationship for life. It is a commercial transaction. Some hires will move on quite quickly, because something else seems like a better proposition. In other cases, founders will be the ones that make that decision, moving people out of the company that are not suitable for the next stage of growth. Not everyone will grow at the same pace as the company.

It is impossible to recruit the *perfect* team. Firstly, there is no such thing. Perfection is impossible. Secondly, it is better to have a range of abilities and personality types. But taking your time over this process will dramatically increase the chances of attracting a good mix of top talent.

Once a candidate has been identified as a good fit, the start-up team needs to move quickly to sign them up. It helps to have all the documentation ready, so a verbal job offer can be followed up with the necessary paperwork and contracts signed.

The next challenge is keeping them.

Managing the team

Founders need to be the equivalent of start-up method actors: permanently in role. Having made the big sale, the job is never over. That war for talent is ongoing, which means we remain in a very competitive jobs market. Good people get offers all the time. Just because new team members were excited enough about the potential of the start-up to join it, doesn't guarantee they are going to stick it out forever, through thick and thin. It is by no means inconceivable that another start-up will come along with an even more compelling sell.

As everyone begins working and the start-up begins to take shape, the person at the top needs to carry on with their sales pitch. Every single day. When they walk into the office, people on the team need to be acknowledged and, where possible, given some words of encouragement, whether it is referring to something that is going on that day or an upcoming presentation.

It is not just about a founder perching on the edge of desks for smiles and laughs. Founders also need to keep on top of pace-setting and relentlessly drive the team forward towards the vision. Just to add to the challenge, though, they also need to perfect the balancing act of pausing long enough to listen to any reservations from individual team members about the direction of travel.

Getting the tone right when it comes to one-to-one communications is key. No one wants to stereotype but, in some circumstances, there is a difference between how men and women communicate and behave. If, as a female founder, you are aware of this and better understand the nuances of behaviour and speech, it can help you to be a more effective leader which will be crucial as the team expands. I learned a huge amount about this from a book called *You Just Don't Understand: Women and men in conversation*, by Deborah Tannen.[1] A good example from it concerns how a woman manages a male team member when she asks him to do something. She can often believe she has to win his full agreement over what needs to be done, in order for it to be carried out in the way she wants it. A man, on the other hand, doesn't consider that there needs to be agreement at all. He may question the logic behind the decision, or even argue about it, but whatever happens, he will still go off and do it because the boss has told him to get it done. In other words, it is completely unnecessary to spend time and energy persuading a male colleague to follow a course of action if they are going to do it anyway. For balance, I will add that when a female report argues about a course of action, she is then more likely not to do it because she has conviction in her position.

Preconceptions about gender work both ways. There may be an expectation that a female CEO would adopt a more caring and nurturing stance. My advice to any female leader who finds themselves expected to offer tea or coffee to the team at the start of the meeting is – don't. Call it out and nip it in the bud.

The most important aspect of whole team communication is to make sure everyone is aware of the vision and their role in achieving it. The nature of a high-growth business is they will all be working flat-out all of the time. It is easy to plough on regardless, without checking in to make sure everything is heading in the right direction. This becomes especially challenging as the numbers begin to swell.

Businesses are relatively straightforward to run when they're made up of fewer than 50 people. There is the bandwidth for everyone to communicate and nothing gets lost. Once the numbers begin to creep up, though, communication doesn't run up and down the company as easily as it used to. When that happens, rumours and toxicity can easily begin to seep in. Valued team members will begin to leave if they don't feel engaged, or can't see their progression. The only way to resolve this is to make sure everyone's very clear on what they need to do and that every single person on the team has a personal progression plan. Running alongside this, everyone needs to see what other groups are doing, so they can align their own progress with it, which is better for everyone in the long run. One of the best ways to do this is to introduce some sort of regular ritual for all-team updates, preferably in a relaxed group setting. One of Starling Bank's most important rituals were our demos, which were held each Friday morning. The developers would do a live demo of our app to show what had been built that week. It was always a lively occasion, where everyone was expected to participate by showing their appreciation, or otherwise, of the progress. Boxes full of bacon butties were delivered from a local café to cater for the team, although as the numbers grew that became impractical. We switched to trade caterers, which was good because they could also accommodate the vegetarian and vegan Starlings.

As the team grows, it might be worth adopting the two-pizza rule, subdividing it into smaller sections for these rituals. This is based on an idea coined by Jeff Bezos, who declared that the smaller the team, the better the collaboration. Imagine a group working late trying to solve an issue and they send out for pizza. The team that only requires two pizzas to feed everyone is the optimal size, deemed to be more efficient than one that needs three to make sure everyone is properly fed. The three-pizza crew will be less agile and communication will be slower.

Bringing in team members is never an excuse for a founder to take their eye off the ball entirely and only think the big thoughts. Quite the opposite, in fact. Aside from the fact that running a lean start-up is very hands-on, there needs to be an awareness that there will always be people on the team aching to chase rainbows, perhaps in a bid to take short cuts to instant fast growth. That is the nature of pulling together a truly entrepreneurial team that is eager to flex their creative muscles. At a very busy time in Starling's growth story, one of the senior team was very keen that we offered support to a company providing services to grassroots football clubs. The brochure he presented looked very compelling, with pictures of football grounds that had been given a makeover to help underprivileged youngsters into the sport. Instinct told me something about it just didn't seem right though. Since we were likely to be on the hook for more than £1 million if we got involved, I decided to make a few calls. On my first call to one of the youth organizations that had allegedly been helped by the initiative, I was told they had no idea of what I was talking about. After further investigation, it transpired that some of the grounds featured in the glossy brochure were not even in the UK. Needless to say, we did not pursue the 'opportunity'.

Even as the team begins to grow, founders can never lose sight of the fact that every single thing that happens to the business will be their responsibility. They have made the hiring decisions, so if hires don't do the job as expected, or progress stalls, it is their call.

Note

[1] D Tannen (1992) *You Just Don't Understand: Women and men in conversation*, Virago, London

CHAPTER SIX

Building the momentum

I t may seem reasonable for founders to want their product or service to be 100 per cent before releasing it into the wider world, so everyone can fully reap the benefits of the idea they've been agonizing over for weeks, months or even more than a year. If they get the launch wrong, all those potential customers might see the new offering as a disaster, and never return. They have, however, been discouraged from this stance. The advice to all start-ups has long been to make a MVP and get it out there asap. In recent times, there have been some dissenting voices. Former ChatGPT CEO Sam Altman says that this viewpoint leads start-ups to launch too early with a mediocre product that can turn off customers because the product doesn't meet their needs. He says finding a smaller group of customers who love a product, rather than 1,000 who are indifferent to it, is far more important. I still err on the side of getting a product out there at the earliest opportunity. The reality is that it takes a lot of time to get noticed at all. This is particularly so for first-time entrepreneurs. No one has heard of them, so no one is dying to try the new product, however innovative.

When Starling Bank went live after receiving our banking licence, we took ages and ages to reach 10,000 customers. We did marketing campaign after marketing campaign, and nothing quite seemed to hit the mark. Each time, we'd be convinced this was going to be *the one* too. We'd be ridiculously enthusiastic, even worrying that too many people would sign up in one go, which would put inordinate pressure on our systems. One time, there was an extensive discussion about whether we should actually go ahead with a mailing to two million subscribers to the Money Saving Expert website. Many of my colleagues tried to talk me out of it altogether. They reasoned that if just 1 per cent signed up, that would be 20,000 customers trying to open an account in a single day, which would more than double our existing customer base. We wouldn't be able to cope, they said. I was persuaded to send out just half a million emails in the first batch. We made sure we were fully staffed up on the day the email went out too. We didn't want there to be any hitches in opening the expected deluge of new accounts once all those subscribers read about Starling Bank.

And how many accounts did we open on the big day? Well it was a couple of hundred at most. No matter how ambitious the plans are for a high-growth venture, it will take time to gain momentum. This doesn't mean that the team can just stand still and wait for the magic to happen though. There is a lot to be done to boost the prospects of the business. First among them is not to delay the launch, in a bid to make sure the product is perfect. It will never be perfect. Ever. Right now, though, it is most important to get it out to the market and to start bouncing ideas off users. Don't worry about wholesale rejection. Most people won't notice, and those that do will be early adopters who are always eager to try something new. The best bit about early adopters is they are a very tolerant bunch.

Powerwalking that makes sense

There is nothing to say a launch needs to be an all-singing, all-dancing pitch to the world. It might make more sense to run a small-scale rollout to validate the business model, and then build slowly from there. It really depends upon the available budget at this stage and the product in question.

Think carefully about early test markets and the users who will be most receptive to it, to give the product the greatest possible chance and generate the most useful feedback. This was the tactic used by Joanna Jensen, when she launched her natural skin care product for children with sensitive and eczema-prone skin in 2012. The potential market was substantial, since one in five children under five suffer with atopic eczema, but she was up against pharmaceutical giants, which marketed products such as Johnson's Baby and Baby Dove. Having created a bespoke product for kids, rather than a mini version of an adult one, Joanna believed she had an advantage. The only way to find out though, was to put her product in the hands of consumers.

It is absolutely vital to understand who your consumer is, and this means you need to engage with your target purchaser before you even think about building up distribution. Once I had developed my first range of six products, I had 1,000 of each made which I took to my eldest daughter's school, and also gave them to family and friends with children. I gave them all a questionnaire, so they could tell me what they thought of the products and their efficacy on children's skin and hair. When I got overwhelmingly positive feedback that the products soothed sensitive and even eczema-prone skin, I went further afield and put samples in the hands of strangers. I had a box of products in the back of my car, so it was not uncommon for me to pass a family in the street, pull over and thrust a bag of samples in their hands to try!

As Childs Farm got more established, I was offered an opportunity to hand out samples at Waterloo Station, but I turned it down. I had no idea what percentage of these commuters had children or participated in bath-time. I wasn't trying to run before I could walk, but I wanted to power-walk in the right direction! So, when I was invited to hand out samples via the National Childbirth Trust, I was all over it as the consumers and end users were our target market.

I was doing everything on a bare minimum budget, but this initial period was still costly. Since these were cosmetic products for children being produced, I couldn't just mix them up on my kitchen table and pop them in a bottle. It had to be done by an established manufacturer authorized to make cosmetic products using a child-friendly (and sustainable) preservative. I had small quantities made up initially, but still spent £15,000 on product that I gave away. When we began making products to sell, I was very lucky that I found suppliers that were very generous with payment terms, letting me pay in 90 days. As time went on, sometimes this stretched to 120 days, or 180 days, or even two-and-a-half years in one case! Whilst I was very convincing with my suppliers, the early consumer legwork I undertook meant they believed in the brand as much as I did, and they knew I had a compelling idea that resonated with consumers and retailers.

Joanna Jensen, Founder, Childs Farm

When things are still relatively low-key, it is a perfect time to start ironing out issues with the tech, supply chain and the product itself. This is also the moment to scrutinize the pricing on the product to find out whether the first customers feel it matches the value it provides. Do they think it is over- or under-priced in comparison to competitive products? Thought can also be given to sales channels. Are customers finding the product easily, or would they expect to see this product available elsewhere?

Yes, the eventual goal is high growth, but for now the priority is refining the offer. This doesn't mean that anyone should lose sight of the vision to scale, but for now it's helpful to think more in terms of growing by 10 per cent a week. If 100 users sign up, aim to get 10 more next week. If a business keeps growing by 10 per cent a week, it's surprising how big the numbers will get. (If it only hits 1 per cent growth per week, it is a sign something is wrong and the team hasn't yet figured out what it is doing.) There is power in small numbers, too. When there's only a handful of customers, it is not difficult to add on a new one which makes the percentage growth look great. That can give the whole team a real lift.

Pivot or tweak

Pivot is a much over-used word in entrepreneurialism. Many start-ups seem to drop the word into conversation liberally, implying they pivot virtually every day. In reality, they are doing what every entrepreneurial venture should be doing: listening to feedback and tweaking their products as they go along. In the true sense of the word, pivoting means *fundamentally changing* the course of the business. Think here of Twitter, which began life as Odeo, a podcast network, but switched to become what was then billed as a micro-blogging platform, closer to the X model we know today. Or Netflix, which pivoted from sending out DVDs in the post to streaming video and even making programmes, after seeing the writing was on the wall for its original business model. Such dramatic pivots are actually quite rare.

Now we've got that straight, let's talk about tweaking. The first iteration of any product is highly unlikely to be right, so entrepreneurs should always be open to change. The changes won't need to all be user-led either. First movers in any market will constantly come across obstacles that slow down their progress, or which stop their products functioning as efficiently as they are designed to do. Very often, there is no real reason for these obstacles, other than that it has 'always been done this way'. Start-ups need to pinpoint these unnecessary processes and pioneer new ways of getting through the bureaucracy.

When we started building the Multiverse platform, we didn't go straight in with all the deep tech stuff. We did everything through Google Forms, Excel spreadsheets and phones. Candidates would come to our website, fill out a form, and then we'd call them up and interview them. After that, we'd invite them into our office to meet them in person. It was crazy stuff, but we kept it as a high touch, manual system, so we could figure out which parts of the process we could automate and the best way to do it.

We saw quite quickly that everything to do with apprenticeships was done on paper. Every candidate, every apprentice, was represented by this massive pack of paper. This looked like it was going to be really difficult to change, because each piece needed a wet signature. There was nothing in the rules that really required this. We spoke with the Education and Skills Funding Agency and asked them if they'd accept electronic signatures. The initial answer was no. We kept on asking, though, and eventually they relented. This was a game-changer for us. Just pushing against the way things were done made all the difference.

Sophie Adelman, Co-Founder, Multiverse and One Garden

Of course, users will also give valuable input. After listening carefully to what they say and looking carefully at the competitive landscape, start-ups should adjust as necessary. Be prepared that this can feel like quite a difficult thing to do, especially once a product is out in the market, even via a soft launch. It is easy to get attached to the first iteration, especially after spending so much time refining it before it was launched in the first place. But everyone needs to think in commercial terms.

The key thing is to get the right product proposition. Without it, a start-up is most likely to fail. You can't be led by your emotions or your passion. You have to be ruthlessly objective. There is a fine art to bringing it all together to get it right, the product design, the commercial opportunity and the competitive landscape. But if you can get that right, then you can start to scale quickly.

Tania Boler, Founder, Elvie

There is a skill to listening to feedback. No start-up should be in a position where they feel they need to change everything on the basis of one comment. One of the most frequent mistakes start-ups make is introducing a product to too small a group of customers. The product is then tweaked according to the likes and dislikes of this small, unrepresentative group. If a business begins to build itself to match the ideals of a tiny subset of customers, it will never become a high-growth business. To scale, it needs to meet the needs of a mass market, whether business or consumer. As a general rule of thumb, it's essential to make sure a significant number of users have highlighted an issue, whether positive or negative, before rushing to change it.

The worst possible approach at this stage is to be overcautious, holding back from making any changes in case something else gets broken along the way. The first thing to say about this is that it *will* most likely happen, one change can expose a host of other bits that need tweaking. But, here is the thing, customers don't mind as much as everyone might assume. People understand when something is innovative and that innovation comes with a cost. For any cutting-edge idea to improve there will always be a certain amount of trial and error. If the customer really liked it when they first tried it, they'll come back to check out the updates. Alternatively, if they were never really that interested, but just tried it because they were a little curious, they are unlikely to become loyal customers anyhow.

Even if a tweak to a product seems *disastrous*, it never matters as much as you think. At this stage, the entrepreneurial venture is still relatively unknown. While the founder and their team will be thinking about it 24/7, most people will have never heard of it. You are not yet on their radar. Don't forget, that's an advantage too. You can try anything you want because no one is really looking. You can also afford to burn customers in the beginning. If you have done it right – been naive and thought big – you can make mistakes. This is the only way to learn; when the rubber hits the road and there are customers with something in their hands. And you learn a lot more from failure than you do success. The guiding principle must be that everything you do is something that will benefit the customer. Think through your customer's lens, not your own.

Engaging with the customer

I've always used public relations to get my ideas out into the field. There was a sugar crisis many years back and the country had run out of sugar, We made a bulk order of those tiny packs of sugar you get in restaurants, added some branding and sent them out in a mail shot. The idea behind them was to send something people wouldn't throw away. There must have been a problem with the packaging because they all arrived broken in very sticky envelopes. My next idea was postcards. Everyone saves them. A friend lived in one of the countries bordering the Mediterranean, so I got her to mail them for me. The message was something along the lines of 'Relax – let Freelance Programmers write your programmes.' It was really effective and encouraged people to try Freelance Programmers.

Dame Stephanie Shirley, Founder, Freelance Programmers

The time will come quite quickly when an entrepreneur will have used up their supply of willing friends and family, and friends of friends, and needs to spread the net more widely. The business is not quite at the stage of the big country-wide, or even worldwide, launch because that will take significant investment, which is something we will cover in the coming chapters. However, it is ready to engage with a larger audience. This means getting its product into the hands of consumers who have no prior connection with the business. This is both for feedback purposes, as discussed in the previous section, and to build the momentum. To do this effectively, there needs to be a concerted effort with PR and marketing.

This is one of the few areas where female founders occasionally do have the advantage over their male counterparts. When it comes to unknown, or up-and-coming, entrepreneurs, the print and broadcast media have a fascination for female entrepreneurs who are building high-growth businesses. This might be because there are so few of them and news organizations always lap up David and Goliath type stories. The same goes for the growing number of entrepreneurial and business podcasts which are often desperate to present female voices to balance their output. It is time consuming speaking to all of these outlets, particularly when there is so much else to attend to, but getting the founder story out there like this is a very useful awareness-raising exercise. It gives any start-up a profile and gets the business on the radar of potential users. It also raises it up above all the thousands of other new enterprises looking for investment, which will be useful in the future when funding rounds begin. When the odds are stacked against you, you need to play to every advantage you have.

It would be remiss of me not to point out the potential downsides to this profile-raising activity, which means such campaigns do need to be carefully managed. The term 'mumpreneur', for example, which is used far too often, has patronizing undertones. It seems to carry with it an implication that women entrepreneurs shouldn't stray too far from the kitchen because they don't stand a chance of being the next Zuckerberg. As time goes on and a female founder's reputation begins to build, she will find herself constantly being compared in a negative fashion to her male counterparts who lead businesses in similar sectors. It's partly tall poppy syndrome: the press spends months and months building up a figure, only to cut them down when they are perceived to have had too much exposure. Experience shows, too, that commentators can be quite judgemental against female-led ventures. There is often a not-too-well-disguised undercurrent of '*Is she up to this?*'

Careful management of the profiles of both the business and the female founder can make a huge difference. There is nothing that can be done to stop negative stories. Remain calm and focused, and always be helpful and charming to journalists even when they seem overly negative. If you rise to the bait, or refuse to engage, they will write what they want to write anyway. It is far better to keep talking. That way, you can make sure that your side of the story is always given some air.

Start to think, also, about all the ways you can engage with your potential customer base on a one-to-one basis through relevant content. The plan should be based around places users are most likely to find the business and be helpful and engaging, rather than a pure sales pitch. I started writing a blog about Starling long, long before we had a product in the hands of customers, years in fact. It was a struggle to write one each week and a huge effort because often I really didn't have very much to say, but it was crucial to keep the momentum.

To begin with, barely anyone noticed, much less read, the blogs. As time went on, I became more adept at creating content that people found interesting. I found that, as a general rule, the stuff that got the most traction was about the fintech, or neo bank, scene as a whole, rather than writing purely about Starling. One of my most successful blogs was an infographic depicting all the players in the market and how they were connected. That was re-tweeted by a number of large organizations such as Accenture and McKinsey. Another blog about the status of Open Banking had a similar impact. Both pieces helped give the Starling domain authority, making people more likely to find us when they Googled 'digital bank' or even just our name. When you can find something interesting and authoritative to say, it drives traffic to your website.

We took the decision very early on to engage with consumers and build trust by becoming *the* information source about pensions. This is how we would gain reach. If anyone was searching online with a question about pensions, we'd have the content they needed. It was all about showing that we could be useful. The content we created was very much aligned with our branding and tone of voice. Maybe people wouldn't be convinced enough to use us when we only had 1,000 customers, but they might be more convinced when we had 100,000 customers, or 200,000 customers because we'd already proven ourselves to be a trusted source.

One of the decisions we made was to take email addresses so we could contact potential customers and serve them content. Again, they may not have been ready to combine their pensions on the first visit to PensionBee to gather information, but they may be in a year's time. Another early strategic decision was to invest in Trustpilot. We made sure that we were very open and transparent about the experiences our customers were getting, responding quickly, in a genuine way, to both good and bad reviews.

Eventually, we moved on to bigger brand channels, such as TV and radio, so we gradually increased our reach over time. The key thing for us was that we knew we had a significant potential customer base since 27 million people have old pensions from previous jobs. It made it worthwhile to invest in these more strategic longer-term initiatives.

Romi Savova, Founder and CEO, PensionBee

When designing communication campaigns, entrepreneurs should think about what it is their company or product does to solve a problem for users. PensionBee's campaign was effective because it provided much-needed commentary on pensions, a subject that can be mystifying to many ordinary people. No one cares about what a company sells, particularly if it is a brand they have never heard of. They are simply interested in better, faster, more effective ways to get what they need. Any product or service is simply a means to an end.

Most times, consumers are fully aware of the problems they have. Or, at least, they have niggling doubts every time they use an existing product or service and it is just not quite right. They may even have a moment of clarity: *wouldn't it be better if?* But, they don't really know how to fully solve the problem, which is why someone coming along and saying 'Hey, I know this is a problem, here is a solution' is so powerful. Thus, any communication campaign needs to prioritize showing potential customers that the answer is right here. Shout it from the rooftops: this amazing start-up has the expertise to make all the pain points go away.

To be effective in this endeavour, the starting point is to identify what the problems are. There may be one, or several, but focus on the biggest one for now. The work that has already been done with early users will be a big help here. Then, rather than focusing on the product, build the campaign around trigger phrases that resonate.

When Multiverse launched, we asked ourselves what do employers need from apprenticeships? If we were going to get employers to pay for an apprentice, their training, and accept the time element of it, we needed to give them something that is better than they already had. The biggest pain point for the employers was that even when they hired graduates, they still had to train them. We put in place a really high-quality training scheme to solve that problem and found them motivated young people to join their apprenticeship schemes.

We also asked young people what was wrong with apprenticeships today. The response was that they were boring and there was no community element to it. Their friends who were at university, meanwhile, were having a great time. Giving up that social experience was a big barrier. Our solution was to create that social experience for our apprentices. Initially, this took the form of a lot of events. Then, we built a community platform so apprentices could ask each other questions and get to know each other, including other Multiverse apprentices in their local area, and they began to form clubs. The solution to this problem was to work with our apprenticeship community to create the experiences they wanted and valued.

Sophie Adelman, Co-Founder, Multiverse and One Garden

CHAPTER SEVEN

Investment – the basics

Raising money is the third, and by far the most difficult, phase of the three phases of a start-up. In the first phase, an entrepreneur has a good idea, but hasn't yet spent any money. Without any sort of commitment, they can easily walk away from it at any time. The pressure increases in the second phase, where they put a little of their own money into the venture. It now feels like there's an obligation to make the venture a success to at least recoup the personal investment, even if the business doesn't grow as much as hoped. The time when it becomes a real point of no return is when *someone else* invests their money into the business. Now there is the additional pressure to give them a return on their investment. In the worst-case scenario, if it all goes badly, the investor may have leverage to kick the founder out of the business altogether.

The additional money required to scale a high-growth business will almost certainly come from outside investors. To remind you, the first rule of successful entrepreneurship is: entrepreneurs don't spend their own money – they spend other people's money. While it is possible to grow some types of businesses to a significant size by simply reinvesting profits, this can be a slow process. It can take many, many years to scale. Think of it this way – high-growth businesses follow a hockey stick profile. There will be time spent, possibly years, developing the brand and building the infrastructure. The goal is to create a model which can support not just a million customers, but 10 million, or even 20 million or more. Then, after all the loss-making years, the business will have the leverage to be a high-growth company.

Funding will be required for those loss-making years, where the solid foundations of a high-growth enterprise are laid. The key to high growth is to propel a business out of the loss-making stage and onto the rapidly rising part of the hockey stick. Very few businesses manage to make this leap.

Convincing others to invest is the most challenging task yet in this journey. Before we look at how to increase the odds of success, let's consider the available options. While there are a lot of funding opportunities open to SMEs, not all are suitable for high-growth businesses.

Funding options

Bootstrapping

The name for this is taken from the old saying 'pulling yourself up by your bootstraps' and refers to entrepreneurs who fund their own ventures entirely from savings, or from money lent to them by friends and family. In most cases, the sums are small. While many SME founders like this approach, because it's straight forward and they retain full control of their business, bootstrapping is the least likely source of funding for a high-growth business, because there simply isn't enough cash invested to scale rapidly.

Bank loans

Another traditional funding route for smaller business is a bank loan. However, mainstream banks are extremely unlikely to lend money to high-growth businesses because of the amounts involved and the fact they are perceived as the riskier option. Even if a bank can be persuaded of the opportunity, they would want security for the loan, such as a claim on the founder's house, so it is a far-from-ideal option.

Grants

There is a bewildering array of grants available for start-ups, and tech-based businesses in particular. Many successful businesses have based their growth strategy on them. It can be quite a detailed and complex process applying for them, but some grant offers run into many millions, which can make a massive difference, particularly in the early days of scaling. Starling Bank built a great deal of its business account offer on the back of a £100 million grant. (The size of the sum was unusual, but the initiative was part of a government drive to reverse many of the bank mega mergers that had been blamed for playing a role in the 2008 financial crisis. However, these opportunities do arise now and again.) Being awarded such a sum, when we had, at the time, raised about the same from investors, was huge. We doubled our funding overnight and didn't have to give away any equity for it. We did, however, have to commit to building the UK's best bank for SMEs, which we did.

It is also well worth getting acquainted with the Enterprise Investment Scheme (EIS), a government-backed scheme to encourage investment in higher-risk, early-stage companies.[1] There are strict criteria around this scheme, including eligibility rules, but on offer is a maximum of £150,000 including state aid, awarded in the three years running up to the date of investment. EIS is attractive for angel investors, because it offers 30 per cent upfront income tax relief to investors, and they are exempt from capital gains and dividends tax. (*Note:* The future of EIS has yet to be decided. At the time of writing, the income incentive is set to expire in April 2025.)

There are many other government grants and incentives geared to promoting growth in particular sectors. R&D tax credits, for example, are available for innovative projects in science and technology. There are also funds available for health initiatives, social care and care of the environment, as well as a large number geared to developing businesses in certain regions. Opportunities can be found on government websites or by talking with trade bodies in relevant sectors.[2]

In most cases, wherever you are in the world grants and funds will not be enough to fund the long-term ambitions of a high-growth business, but they may be able to sustain it while it is seeking large cash injections elsewhere.

Crowdfunding

Crowdfunding has grown in popularity in recent years, and there are a number of platforms dedicated to helping businesses raise money by asking a large amount of people to contribute small amounts online. This was the route taken by Monzo, which secured £1 million of investment in a record-breaking 96 seconds via Crowdcube. The bank had already raised £7 million via Passion Capital. The reason this was seen to be such a success was, as well as the £1 million, the raise created a real buzz around the brand ahead of its launch. BrewDog is another brand that has used crowdfunding very effectively in this way.

While access to a large and diverse pool of enthusiastic backers has its advantages in building demand, it does come with its challenges. Any business that chooses this route will be competing against thousands of other projects seeking crowdfunding. Perhaps more importantly, if it does succeed, it will now have potentially hundreds of shareholders. They will expect regular communication, full transparency and be impatient that promises are kept within expected timelines.

Angel investment

Angel investors, also known as business angels, or seed investors, put their own money into businesses in exchange for shares in the company. They can work individually, or as part of a network to create a larger investment pool. Many angels have interests in particular sectors or regions. As noted above, angel investments are often combined with EIS opportunities. Romi Savova, who took this route with a number of angel rounds to raise investment for PensionBee, says EIS was a 'game changer' and raised the conversion rate for angel pitches.

We took quite an unusual route to raising money. We started by raising through angels, and had a fairly sizable first round, raising around £1 million. It was a lot, but we are a regulated pensions business and needed that sum. We continued to raise angel money after that through a network of individuals I'd worked with before, or knew from my previous jobs.

Romi Savova, Founder and CEO, PensionBee

Angel investments are often talked about as an alternative to venture capital funding. It is, however, important to note that Romi's first round is the exception to the rule and the sums involved are generally far smaller. Angel investors typically invest between £10,000 and £50,000, although it is possible they will go as high as £150,000.[3] The smallest VC investments begin at £100,000, but can rise well into the millions.

Many start-ups use angels for seed funding, which can be considered as the first official cash injection. The idea is to put in enough money so the business can be built to a size that establishes a proof of principal to take it to the next, more significant funding round. Some businesses will scale by taking repeated rounds of angel funding, but will grow at a far slower pace.

Family offices

Starling's first investment was from a family office. Family offices are private wealth management advisory firms that look after the money of high net worth individuals, creating investment funds of £30 million plus. Some of the wealth managers that manage the funds have a reputation for being quite eccentric, but what makes the idea quite interesting is these funds are known to have broader investment criteria than most VCs. VCs will specify which categories of company they'll invest in, how much can be put in a single investment and even the preferred type of founder, whereas family offices rarely have rules. The approach is far more flexible, because they only have to answer to themselves.

Something that founders may find interesting is that family offices are often happy to play the long game. Typically, VC funds will only hold funds for three to five years, because they want a rapid exit to recoup their (hopefully vastly increased) stake and enhance their credentials. Success in this endeavour will lead to their next, ideally larger, fund. Family offices are not so beholden to this tight funding cycle and will often be happy to stick around for double the amount of time.

Venture capital

VCs invest in portions of a company at various stages of its operation, with a view to a big exit via an IPO down the line, or selling it to another business for a profit. Their model is built around spotting and backing successful high-growth businesses. Any R&D heavy, or very technical, businesses that need a large injection of money before they can begin to trade will almost certainly need VC help, but other businesses seeking to scale rapidly will be hard pushed to find a more effective route.

The odds of getting VC funding are tiny. In fact, it is estimated that just 0.05 per cent of start-ups are successful.[4] We already know that, of that tiny amount, all-female founding teams secure just 2 per cent of VC investment.[5] Since even putting yourself forward for investment is a hugely high-risk endeavour, it pays to get informed ahead of time.

Understanding the VC model

VC funds are raised from wealthy individuals who are often former investment bankers, pension funds and even ex-entrepreneurs. Each investment partner that puts in a certain amount to a fund gets an asset allocation according to the percentage they put in. VCs will charge their investment partners 2 per cent of the fund in admin fees and take a percentage of the fund profits, usually around 20 per cent.

When it comes to allocating money from these funds, VCs see hundreds of start-ups, although there are many who never even get seen. Out of 150 pitches, they'll invite a small handful back for further talks, but not all will get an offer.

Now, imagine 10 start-ups that beat all the odds to get that offer. VCs accept that there is a likelihood that three of that number will crash and burn, possibly quite quickly. A further four will limp along, getting nowhere close to the lofty forecasts made at the pitch and will eventually be sold for less than the original investment. Two more investments will do OK, but will not make back the VC anything more than twice the initial stake. That leaves one solitary investment to be the superstar of the whole bunch. All being well, this extraordinary start-up will soar in value to yield 10x return, known as a 'venture rate of return'. For, say, a £10 million investment, the VC would get back £100 million. VCs are so choosy because this £100 million needs to cover all the money put into the investments that didn't realize anything like they were expected to, or even nothing at all. This is also probably why investors tend to get hamstrung by looking for patterns, other investments that are similar to runaway successes. When Amazon began to gain traction, it is certain that the business model of other online bookstores got a bit more attention at the pitch stage. Likewise, when Uber and Lyft started to accelerate away, investors were undoubtedly more receptive to different types of taxi operations. If anyone else's business doesn't fit into that pattern, it can be an uphill battle to convince investors that this will be the *next* pattern.

I often picture the process like a music industry talent scout looking for the next big act. They will have to sit through thousands of performances of mediocre singers until they find the next Madonna. Is it worth it? Of course it is, because getting in at the start, while the next Madonna is an unknown, will be a huge, huge money spinner. Meanwhile, though, many talented acts will slip under the radar.

What is equally galling for start-ups is how ruthless this process can be even if they are feted as the next Madonna. Any business that beats the odds and gets an investment might feel that they've taken a huge stride forward – and they have. However, things can change in the blink of an eye. Part of the VC package is that experienced investors share the benefit of their knowledge to help a start-up navigate their path to high growth. Rest assured, the second that there is a sign, however vague, that a start-up is not progressing as it should, that support will instantly be withdrawn. VCs will not waste any time, or capital, on trying to drag along weak businesses. It sounds brutal, because it is.

> When I first started pitching, I didn't really understand the way that funds work. I didn't know that they might invest in 20 companies and that, basically, if yours is not performing in the top three, it will just be discarded. By discarded, I don't mean immediately got rid of. The investor will follow along, but they won't invest their time and effort into it, to help you along the road.
>
> Founders need to understand things from the investment standpoint. If you get investment, the partner you work with has to answer to other partners, and the managing partner. This means, you really need to look at the fund as a whole and how well it is doing elsewhere.
>
> **Alex Depledge, Founder and CEO, Resi**

If the bleak odds presented here don't put founders off, there is something else to consider. I've hinted at it in the previous paragraph when I said that VCs share the benefit of their knowledge. While in some cases this is welcome, in others it is not. Working with a VC means ceding a huge amount of control. A question all founders need to ask themselves is this: do you want to be a master of your own destiny, i.e. in control, or are you prepared to give that up for a greater chance of financial success? It is not an easy one to answer. Yes, VC funding can provide rocket fuel to any business, but there will also be a high probability that a VC will want a seat on the board and to get very close to the day-to-day management of the business. If this is not something a founder feels they can be comfortable about, then they will need to accept that they will grow more slowly, with smaller sources of investment, such as angel investors, or even slower if they choose to scale organically. With the latter option, it is far more likely that any firm will only ever remain a small business.

Why the odds are stacked against female founders

The sections above could apply to *any* entrepreneur seeking investment, regardless of gender. However, as we know, female founders are considerably less likely to secure backing than their male counterparts. It is worth exploring some of the reasons behind that to help female founders prepare for what can be a very challenging time ahead.

Most entrepreneurs entering the pitch process will quickly realize that investment management is a very male-dominated sector. Many private equity and venture capital investment committees don't include a *single* female investor. If entrepreneurs knew just how imbalanced it is, they'd most likely be shocked. It was only in 2015 that anyone tried to measure the proportion of females in senior investment posts in private equity. In the UK a dozen women working in senior private equity roles got together to found a non-profit organization called Level 20 in a bid to improve gender diversity in the sector. One of their first initiatives was to measure the extent of the issue, on the grounds that if you can't measure it, you can't manage it. Helen Steers, a Level 20 co-founder, said she was horrified by the findings.

Only 6 per cent of senior investment roles in private equity were held by women in 2015. Today, that figure is around 10 per cent, which is still not nearly enough and only halfway to our core objective to reach 20 per cent. There is a big job to do. Younger women who might consider a career in private equity and venture capital can be put off by the scarcity of female role models, so the imbalance continues.

When you have a bunch of people of the same gender, or the same ethnic or socio-economic background, they are much more susceptible to group-think. When everyone thinks the same way, there is less questioning and that is where mistakes get made. Yet, performance is absolutely key in this sector of the investment universe. What this industry needs to understand is that performance will be better if there is a more diverse set of people making investment decisions and participating in the value creation phase of portfolio companies.

Through our work at Level 20 we've raised this bias with some male investors and they generally don't recognize the unconscious biases they have, or might be showing. Voicing the issue does hit home though, particularly among those that have daughters. They can see things need to change. It's reverse mentoring.

It's an important issue from a social perspective too. Much of the money into our sector comes from pension funds, insurance companies and investment management firms, who all care about diversity and inclusion. My own role at Pantheon, which has around $90 billion in assets under management and advice, is to commit to private equity and venture capital funds, co-invest alongside these funds in deals and manage the investments for our clients. We have strong diversity credentials ourselves (over 40 per cent of senior roles at Pantheon are held by women) and push back strongly with our fund managers if we don't see any attempt at diversity.

Helen Steers, Partner, Pantheon

It is very easy to see how this group-think manifests itself. Each pitch to a VC is made to an individual partner, who needs to be persuaded that the start-up or growth business in front of them has a great idea. (Their more junior associates may join the meeting too.) If this is the case, they then need to take this idea to their organization's investment committee to green light it. This is where the issue with investing in 'people like us' really begins. If you are a 30-something guy who wears designer jeans, you are most likely to invest in another 30-something guy who wears designer jeans, because you think they're cool. You (the cool, jean-wearing 30-year-old) would be far less likely to champion a 40- or 50-something woman, because you have absolutely nothing in common, so don't see them as cool. Who would want to take something to their seniors they don't believe to be cool? It's not an easy sell to themselves, so it just represents hard work.

I am fairly certain that one of the main reasons Starling struggled to get funding for so long was because of me. It wasn't just that I was a woman either. I also didn't fit into the obvious entrepreneur box. I'd had a lengthy previous career in corporate life, and I was five feet tall and Welsh. VC partners would often address questions about technology to my colleagues, despite my making it clear that I was perfectly comfortable with it. My degree is in computer science, and I studied artificial intelligence years before most people had even heard of it. Investors found all this difficult because they didn't see other entrepreneurs like me, so didn't really have any frame of reference. If there is one thing investors like, it is for things to be predictable.

I am not the only female founder to have had this sort of experience.

We pitched to 30 VCs in London and 15 in the north of England, and there was not a single female partner at any of the pitches.

As a female founder running a tech company in the north of England, it was very, very difficult to get the attention of funds, especially those based in London. You aren't like them, you are in a place that they don't know and they have no sense of the talent ecosystem in Leeds. They don't even know how long it would take on the train to get there. Also, because you aren't in their networks or circles in London, they've never heard of you. You're placed in the 'hard box' from day one. Right from the start, I was in a position where I not only had to sell myself and my business, but I also had to sell my city.

One investor said to me: 'Isn't it all coal mines and textiles in Leeds?' Another asked if there were even any tech businesses in Leeds.*

I've had people all but ask who's pulling the strings. They'll look over my shoulder to see if anyone else is there. When I started talking to one VC, he stared into his laptop. Yet, when my male CTO spoke, he'd look up. In the end, it got quite farcical. The VC would ask a question and I'd answer and then he'd pose the exact same question to the CTO. My CTO spoke up and asked if the VC minded closing his laptop and addressing his questions to the CEO who was also, clearly, in the room. It went downhill from there. The investor was so rude we had to leave.

I'd do it differently now. I'd start from the position of accepting that there are these barriers, whether it is gender, or geographic. Then, I would bring it out into the open and talk about it. I think we need to shout about our credentials and personal brand values more, and become confident about talking about ourselves as experts and thought leaders.

Men do this as a matter of course. They talk strongly about themselves and are very confident about it. It feels uncomfortable at first but sometimes we do need to step into some uncomfortable places to get what we want. Ultimately though, it comes down to how much you really believe in your business.

Zandra Moore, Founder and CEO, Panintelligence

(*There are, including Leeds-based TransUnion, which is a major player in the fintech world, Sky Betting and Gaming and its parent company Flutter, which is a huge technology play. Also, the north of England was home to Pipex, the UK's first commercial internet service provider, established in 1990.)

Moves are afoot to boost female representation among the senior ranks of investors, thanks to campaigning organizations such as Level 20. The challenge is that VC firms run on an apprenticeship-style model. Associates start in junior positions and then move up the ranks as they gain experience. It is not possible to parachute women into the senior ranks to become partners, however high-powered their careers have been elsewhere. Right now, we are at the stage where many more women are being welcomed into the more junior ranks of VCs, taking analyst and associate roles, but it will take time for them to progress through the levels to reach senior positions. Those who have reached senior positions are also working hard to advocate for their female colleagues.

I take great pains to make sure women have a voice in our internal meetings. I will go around the room and ask: 'What do you think of this deal?' When they give their response, I acknowledge it and say, 'That's a really helpful point.' It shows other women on the team that I have their back. Senior women should advocate for junior women like this. It is not a competition. There's more than enough space for all of us.

If I do feel the need to call out unfairness when I see it, I'll make it into a joke, but I will be sure to make the point. If, say, someone declares a pitch is 'great', and represents the 'perfect deal', I'll always point out that it is not, in fact, perfect because there are no women on the team.

Deepali Nangia, Partner, Female and Diverse Founders, Speedinvest

For female founders at the start of this process, there's a lot to weigh up. Once armed with the basics, it's helpful to supplement the knowledge by speaking to other entrepreneurs who have already been through the process to further explore the implications.

We would always tell any founder who wants to work with us to speak to others we've worked with. They need to know what it is really like to work with us – the good, the bad and the ugly. I encourage them to ask what happened when things go wrong. Do other founders believe their investment team have been there by their side? Were they supportive? This should be done a long time before signing, so everyone knows what to expect.

June Angelides, VC, Samos Investments

Things are changing, but it will take time. For now, for whatever reasons, certain investors will harbour views that a female founder isn't really leading the company and doesn't really understand what is going on. There are always going to be men who find it much easier to have conversations with other men, rather than a woman. While it can be difficult to accept, since each VC meeting feels a huge part of the start-up journey, it is not. There will be dozens and dozens of VC meetings, possibly even hundreds. Female founders, indeed all founders, will leave empty-handed from the vast majority. The investors who disregarded a female founder's input, or who felt more comfortable speaking to their male colleagues, will have forgotten about them less than an hour after they left the room. They'll most likely never realize their behaviour was out of order. Even if they did know they were being deliberately offensive, it doesn't matter. Or, at least, it shouldn't matter to the founder, particularly if it matters so much that it impacts their performance at the next meeting.

Perhaps it is easier for female founders to think about it in this way: each of us as individuals are not there to change the world, unless it is with the amazing product or service we are bringing to market. Your aim is to get funding for your start-up, to build the business and to be a successful CEO.

While there are numerous injustices in the world, others who are currently in a better position to do so are fighting to even the playing field. Leave it up to them. For now, focus on finding and speaking with investors that do value you and what you have to say. Once you do get funding, you will be on the way to reaching a position where you can say whatever you want!

Notes

[1] HM Revenue and Customs. Apply to use the Seed Enterprise Investment Scheme to raise money for your company, Gov.uk, 16 June 2017. www.gov.uk/guidance/venture-capital-schemes-apply-to-use-the-seed-enterprise-investment-scheme (archived at https://perma.cc/6SDD-LVQK)

[2] Department for Business and Trade. Finance and support for your business, Gov.uk, nd. www.gov.uk/business-finance-support (archived at https://perma.cc/ZMK2-373N)

[3] Halkin. Everything you need to know about angel investors in the UK, Halkin, nd. www.halkin.com/post/angel-investors (archived at https://perma.cc/J6SV-X9PX)

[4] M Grossman. As a new business what are the odds of getting venture capital funding, Techstars, nd. techstars.blog/venture-capital/as-a-new-business-what-are-the-odds-of-getting-venture-capital-funding (archived at https://perma.cc/NZM3-QNE8)

[5] S de Bruin and M Munoz. European women in VC, IDC, May 2022. europeanwomeninvc.idcinteractive.net/104 (archived at https://perma.cc/4HQG-ERAS)

CHAPTER EIGHT

Preparation for an investment round

How far down the road with an idea do you need to be before setting up meetings with investors? It is easy to assume that there needs to be an MVP, at the very least, but this isn't necessarily so. Very often, founders will speak with investors at the very early stages. Having done the research with the initial prototypes, and identified the customer base and suppliers, they are ready to take it to the next stage. An investment round is not, however, something that can be rushed into. As the previous chapter showed, the odds are against success, which means preparation and due diligence are key and this should begin long before the first investor meetings are set up.

> I often feel I have more patience than other investors, which may be something to do with having children. However, even I baulk at someone coming to me with an idea and a blank sheet of paper. I like to see that they have prepared well and have the numbers to hand. Telling me you will figure it out is not enough.
>
> **Deepali Nangia, Partner, Female and Diverse Founders, Speedinvest**

When it comes to meeting investors, it is easy to make a lot of mistakes early on. When I started out, I arranged meetings with funds that invested £300 million to £400 million, when in fact I was looking for a fraction of that amount. This was partly because, in my previous world as a corporate banker, I had dealt with sums that large on a day-to-day basis. Somehow, the disparity between what I needed – just a few million at that stage – and what they were investing in didn't really occur to me. It was only once it was pointed out to me that there are VCs that specialize in investments in the low millions that I changed tactics. The new group of VCs I spoke with were a lot more receptive to my pitch because I was asking for amounts that were in their usual ballpark.

When choosing my list of early targets, I also looked carefully at VCs that had declared loudly that they were working to address the gap in investment in female-led start-ups. The disparity in funding expectations between male- and female-led businesses was just beginning to be talked about more at that time. Many VCs wrote blogs and social media posts announcing that they were actively addressing the issue. For a brief moment, I even toyed with the idea that it might actually be *easier* to be a female founder, since so many VCs were talking about targets. I quickly discovered this was not the case. Talk is cheap, and as far as I could tell made no difference whatsoever. Even if things have improved markedly since, investors won't invest money into a business run by a female founder just because they are female founders. Their number one criterion remains to create the highest return because they have a fiduciary duty to their own investors.

Entrepreneurs also need to be aware that VCs tend to be drawn towards investments in particular market sectors, whether information technology, healthcare, finance or consumer goods and services. Therefore, founders must pitch to a VC that is interested in the appropriate sector, rather than one that has thus far no track record at all with the type of products or services in question.

> Doing your homework is really important. It makes no sense for a small software business to pitch to a mid-market buyout fund that is investing in traditional industrial sectors. If you can find out what else is in their books, it helps to think about the hook for these investors and what it is they are interested in. This helps structure the pitch to hit all the right points.
>
> **Helen Steers, Partner, Pantheon**

The ideal investor needs to be passionate about the mission of a company, which means they have to fully understand the problem that it is trying to solve and how it will solve it. If an entrepreneur must explain this in detail at first, it will be a struggle to get any further.

> We don't have any specialized tech funds in the north of England. The investment community are all generalists. It's hard to pitch a tech company into a generalist fund. Then there's the added challenge of educating the investment community about what a high-growth tech company investment looks like, versus a more bricks-and-mortar type investment where there are assets. Tech businesses are looking at a valuation based on potential profitability. I hadn't appreciated any of that until I went into the process of raising money, and I really felt it.
>
> **Zandra Moore, Founder and CEO, Panintelligence**

A good early source of information is the British Private Equity and Venture Capital Association (BVCA).[1] The BVCA publishes a member directory, where it is possible to search investor details that include where they are located, the types of investments they are interested in and any sector specializations. There is a fee, £150 at the time of writing, but it is a good starting point. LinkedIn can be helpful, too. Use the advanced filtering options to locate investors that are interested in specific sectors.

Another really useful tactic is to look at other business with similar products targeting the same market, but which are a little ahead in their development. These are businesses that may have succeeded in gaining investment a year or so before. There are plenty of sources online, such as TechCrunch, which will give more detail on the funding round via its online CrunchBase service that often includes the size of the investment. Founders shouldn't get put off that these other companies were asking for a lot more than they are currently seeking, or even much less. These are the investment groups that they need to get plugged into too. There are also VC–founder 'speed dating' type events, which can be helpful, although these won't appeal to everyone, and a number of VC podcasts.

This is also the time to get to grips with investor lingo very quickly. This is a market that talks in terms of pre-seed, seed, and series A, B, C and D rounds, with the size of the investment rising at each stage. When an investor promotes itself as prioritizing B and C rounds up to a value of £x, there is little point approaching them with a pitch for pre-seed at a fraction of the amount. Also, being able to speak in the same language as investors is the most efficient way to share information. It is great to articulate a passionate explanation of an idea, but founders who are unable to discuss their equity plan for future B, C and D funding rounds may find investors challenging their expertise and ability to achieve high growth.

Getting an introduction

Once a likely investment partner has been pinpointed, the challenge is to get a meeting with them. While VCs are increasingly letting entrepreneurs pitch direct through their websites, where founders can upload their pitch deck to be reviewed, not all offer this facility. Many VCs will still only operate via 'warm introductions', which is where someone within their network introduces them to an entrepreneur looking for funding. Or, to put it more succinctly: investors don't want to *meet* you, they want to be *introduced* to you. To the VC community, this probably makes a lot of sense. Their role is akin to finding a needle in a haystack. The warm introduction system puts the onus on their network to do the pre-vetting. Unfortunately, it doesn't make as much sense to those trying to get in front of investors and, frustratingly, can put many female founders at a disadvantage from a number of standpoints. They may not have an extensive network that can introduce them to VCs because it often all comes down to going to the right school/university, or moving in the same circles. It is also quite probable that, at this stage, they have not met many other founders. However dedicated we are to networking, it is not always easy to strike up a rapport with other founders who have already received investment. Firstly, the ones that are funded don't tend to attend the same events as those who have not yet got to that point. Secondly, as per the previous chapter, almost all those who have received funding are men. As a 50-something woman when I started out, I know first hand that it is not easy to start a rapport with 30-something male founders. And you do need that easy rapport in order to persuade them to introduce you to their investors.

The approach I developed was to send out emails to all my target investors, using the connections I did have. The goal was to be succinct and give just enough detail to whet their appetite:

Hi* Phil,

I'm seeking funding for my start-up which is going to revolutionize the banking market. I've already got a banking application midstream and am having lots of positive interest in the market. Any chance of a meeting?

(*When I started, I always used to write 'dear so-and-so'. However, my colleagues told me this was far too old-fashioned. Everybody in the start-up world says 'Hi', or, if you are really cool, 'Hey'. I have mastered using 'Hi', but have never managed to bring myself to address anyone with 'Hey'.)

Take care not to exaggerate your prospects, or how far the start-up has come to date. There is such a thing as misrepresentation, so stick to the facts. Also think carefully about directly name-dropping any associates that are already on board to give added credibility. Early in the Starling story, I received interest from a very well-known senior figure on the technology scene. He'd been very helpful and kindly gave me a large amount of advice, as well as access to some of his firm's resources. After seeking permission, I noted this in many of my introductory emails, writing something along the lines of 'Starling is already working closely with {Named Person}, the founder of {Big Tech Firm}.' What I didn't realize at the time was that this actually *put off* a number of investors. The tech firm in question was over three decades old. In tech terms, that's a lifetime. The investors were on the look-out for something cutting edge and new. By emphasizing the name of the established associate, I was sending the subliminal message that Starling was steeped in the past. Why invest with me, when they could meet with 24-year-olds who knew all the buzzwords?

Some start-ups worry that if they send out too many emails in one go, they will be inundated with meetings and won't be able to cope. Don't worry – this is a highly unlikely outcome. And if this does happen, so much the better.

It is all about creating momentum. We were careful to get all our ducks in a row around our pitch, the data room was ready, everything. Then we targeted all our tier one investors, the ones we really wanted, at the same time and booked them all in, back-to-back, over the course of a few days. It was exhausting, but the idea was to get a quick no, learn from the feedback and adjust our pitch for the next meeting.

The VC space is quite insular. There's a lot of chit-chat. You don't want to become known as the start-up that has been at it for months. You want to be surrounded by a feeling of energy and momentum, to keep pushing forward. VCs are status-driven, too, so if one is positive, mention it to another. Create the impression that this deal is hot.

The biggest mistake founders make is to try to pace themselves. It's much better to have an exhausting two-and-a-half weeks and then get on with the job of building the business.

Sophie Adelman, Co-Founder, Multiverse and One Garden

For full disclosure, Starling *was* that start-up that was at it for months. In fact, our first fundraise took two years. Which all goes to show, perseverance is key.

As per the earlier email strategy, if there is no response from an investor, send the email again. Or send it to another partner in the firm who might find it interesting. It sounds like a gruelling slog, and it is, but this is an area where female founders can and do have the upper hand. From an early age, girls have a reputation for diligence. We work effectively and get the job done, which is why schoolgirls are often head-and-shoulders out in front of their male counterparts. That quality doesn't just disappear. Our ability to work efficiently and process data is another one of our superpowers.

There is no doubt in my mind that one of the reasons why Starling did eventually find investors is because I sent one hundred times more emails than anyone else. When I was told very early on that I would need to speak with *at least* 300 investors to gain funding, I resolved to speak to at least 300 investors if that was what it took. (And it did.) I knocked on more doors and had more meetings. Ultimately, so much progress in business is a numbers game – the more people you speak to, the better you get on.

I was thinking about this when I spoke at a seminar put on by a leading law firm. The panel was made up of a mixture of women and men. Each of the women had a stack of notes in front of them, having clearly prepared meticulously. They had interesting content to share too. The majority of the male panellists did not. What did this tell me? It made me think that all this talk about imposter syndrome is nonsense. Women are not just good enough. They are overqualified. Everyone should be listening to hear what they have to say.

This doesn't mean that to get to the top we won't need to be thick skinned. However, once we acknowledge that we have the talent to succeed it is a lot easier to navigate around the brickbats and be relentless. When we focus on getting the job done, we will get it done.

If the emails don't seem to be working, we can always use another of the most important characteristics in any entrepreneur's armoury: the ability to hustle. There is nothing stopping entrepreneurs from contacting other founders who they don't know, to ask for warm intros. Most founders are willing to help fellow founders, provided they are asked in the right way. It can reflect well upon them if they introduce a compelling business to their network. Again, the key here is to really sell your own business. You want them to be excited about your idea. Or, failing that, think of a novel strategy to get an investor to sit up, take notice and agree to a meeting.

One female founder just turned up at my office and I took the meeting. She got 10 out of 10 for hustle and I had to respect that. In another instance, I received a LinkedIn message from a female founder. She'd reached out to me completely cold. What was interesting was she said she'd looked at my portfolio and could see I had invested in this and that, and she'd love to talk to me about a business she was building in a similar sector. I said, 'Great, email me your pitch deck.' That whole approach and the fact she'd taken time to research what I was interested in made my life easier. It felt authentic too.

Female founders who do get in front of investors shouldn't be afraid to ask for a warm intro from them either. If a particular investor says the pitch is not right for them, perhaps because of a conflict with their portfolio, and they seemed to like what they hear, ask them if they can put you in touch with other investors in their network. If they do, stay in touch. This person is now your ally. You have a relationship, and should take time to develop it. If they make the introduction, feed back to them on how it went. They've shown that they want to help you and have a genuine interest.

Deepali Nangia, Partner, Female and Diverse Founders, Speedinvest

There is a possibility that, if female founders make enough noise about their venture, investors may come to them. Many of the new generation of diverse funds are tackling the underrepresentation in investment in certain sectors by seeking out suitable enterprises which are run by founders who are often overlooked. Ada Ventures, under co-founder Check Warner, set up a network of 13 scouts back in 2018. This number has now grown to more than a hundred.

The idea is to flip the warm intro model on its head. Instead of funds saying 'You need to know us to approach us' the scouts create outbound links into underrepresented communities. Around a third of the companies in Ada's first fund came through this network.

Importantly, this network is truly diverse and intersectional as we know that the women who face most barriers to raising money tend to be women of colour, women from more deprived socio-economic backgrounds and women who come from other minoritized communities.[2]

Check Warner, Co-Founder and Partner, Ada Ventures

If an investor shows any interest, there may be a temptation to ask them to sign an NDA ahead of the meeting. Don't. Until you have a real business, no one is going to sign an NDA just to look at it with a view to invest. You will not get meetings if you insist on an NDA.

Some founders might view forgoing an NDA as too much of a leap of faith. But, once again, they must remind themselves that it is not about the idea, it is about the execution. Remember, there are very few original ideas. Investors will be betting on the founder, because they think they are the person to get this product to market.

What any entrepreneur will need to prepare themselves for is the fact that once they begin pitching, their deck will get out, whether or not NDAs are in place. About three months after I first started doing the rounds of investors with Starling's deck, I met up with the founder of another digital bank that was also doing the investment rounds. We'd always got on well and had spoken a few times over the years as we both worked to get our ventures off the ground. I started to tell him how the funding process was going, when he responded brightly that he knew exactly how it was going because various investors had sent him three copies of our pitch deck already.

How much to ask for

Before a founder goes to a single meeting, it is crucial that they know exactly how much they are asking for. There is a lot involved in company valuations. The priority is to get enough cash to get to the next stage, which could be to make the product and get it into the hands of customers, so it can begin making an income. By this time, there should be a fairly clear idea of what this amount will be, not least because it is impossible to make sound financial decisions without this knowledge. The 'ask' from investors will be based on how much cash will be needed to get it to the next stage.

It's easy to fall into the trap of thinking that by aiming high, well above the figure required, it will make a start-up seem more valuable. However, it can also come across as faintly ridiculous if the sum clearly isn't warranted. We are all familiar with the *Dragons' Den* scenario where start-ups with a distinctly underwhelming product and a tiny potential market airily announce they are prepared to 'give away' 10 per cent of their company for £5.5 million pounds. Let's say, though, that this ambitious strategy works. Asking for and getting too much sounds like a nice problem to have. It isn't.

It means the start-up is more likely to be over-valued, which will lead to problems down the road during further rounds of investment. Investors will be reluctant to put money into a business that is overvalued too. There is also a danger that, with so much cash sloshing around, the business will become reliant on investor money. This makes it difficult to pivot, or make any significant changes that may be needed.

The alternative is to go low, in the hope it will attract investors because the sum sounds doable, even with the risk involved in betting on an unknown business. If the ask is too low, though, the company risks running out of money before its products get out into the market and it will have to go through another costly and time-consuming funding round. Plus, without the necessary backing, there might be a temptation to cut corners, or even slow down the scale-up. Investors will notice it too, and take it as a bad sign.

> I always ask myself if they are asking for enough capital. If they are not asking for enough, they won't meet the necessary milestones. This will have a detrimental impact on future funding rounds. On this basis, would this person be able to raise again? Will they be able to build enough traction to make it an obvious investment?
>
> **June Angelides, VC, Samos Investments**

Once again, think about the ask in terms of VC lingo. Investors will expect founders to fully understand how much money they want and at what valuation. This needs to be presented in terms of 'pre' or 'post'. Pre is the valuation of the business *before* the money goes in, and post is the valuation *after* the cash injection. Thus, if an entrepreneur says they are 'trying to raise £3 million on a £24 million pre' it means the business is currently valued at £24 million. If they don't make this clear, and the implication is that it is £24 million post, they could lose £3 million at a stroke.

On my first rounds with Starling, I was raising £3 million on a £9 million pre. In other words, giving away 25 per cent of the company for a £3 million investment. By the time I got to my first big investment, some time later, I raised £48 million on a £72 million pre.

Whatever number is being asked for, investors need to see that there is a clear path to high growth and profit.

Founders need to paint a picture of scale. The biggest reason we say no to founders is because their business is just not going to return the 10x that we need because we have to have lots of failures. Every company needs to have the *potential* to return the fund.

I would also advise anyone not to be afraid of saying how big they feel this thing could grow. If someone tells me they are building a multi-billion dollar company, that makes me sit up and listen. They won't get laughed out of the room. That is what VCs want to hear.

Check Warner, Co-Founder and Partner, Ada Ventures

The percentage of equity given up in return for an investment will vary according to the deal. Variables that will impact the amount include the number of investors and any equity stakes previously awarded in seed rounds.

Notes

[1] British Private Equity and Venture Capital Association. www.bvca.co.uk (archived at https://perma.cc/4KMU-JU9T)

[2] S Kunthara. Black women still receive just a tiny fraction of vc funding despite 5-year high, Crunchbase, 16 July 2021. news.crunchbase.com/diversity/something-ventured-black-women-founders (archived at https://perma.cc/TMX3-Q4WN)

CHAPTER NINE

Creating the pitch

Investors see thousands of pitch decks a year, so it feels like the pressure is on to create the perfect one. In fact, if you Google 'pitch decks' the word 'perfect' comes up time and again. Without a perfect pitch deck, it is impossible to get funding, is the clear implication. The best advice for any founder is to take some of the pressure off themselves and to make their deck *the best it can be*. They should, of course, commit to continually improving it, but at the same time accept it will never, ever be perfect. If you feel in anyway unsure about this, give yourself a break, spend a bit more time online and search out the pitch decks from what are now some of the world's largest companies. There is a lot to be learned from viewing other pitch decks but, in this case, it is also heartening to see how naive some of them were. It shows that we all have a chance.

A first pitch deck will most likely include anything from 8 slides to 50. As a company grows and the ask gets bigger, the deck will grow correspondingly. Founders should use the questions they're asked at each pitch to adjust their decks. Investor questions give valuable clues about what is important to those weighing up whether to fund a venture.

One of the real bonuses of writing a slide deck is it really sharpens one's focus on what the business is all about and what the team is going to deliver. And this delivery should be the main focus of your efforts when writing it. One of the mistakes I made when I started on Starling's first deck was being obsessed with the closing page, and I spent far too long on it. This was the last page of the deck which showed all the small print that covered off the regulatory bits and various caveats. The obligatory part that says 'this is not an offer of securities', and so on. My preoccupation with the closing page was down to my background in corporate banking. I was extremely wary about getting sued for not getting something quite right. For a long time, far too long really, there wasn't anything in the *middle* of the deck.

The elements of a pitch deck

To begin with, let's just briefly outline the elements that need to be included in a pitch deck.

The cover slide

Include the company name, logo and social media handles, against a branded backdrop, either using the corporate colours, or a suitable image. Do not date the cover page. Sooner or later, you will forget to adjust it for the next pitch and it will look dated.

If you are nervous about the pitch finding its way to a competitor, water-mark the cover slide.

Summary

This should be concise, impactful summary of what the business does and its mission. It should be intriguing but not vague. One of the issues with a summary is that when you boil a business down to its basics, it can look rather like the incumbent. We could have said, 'Starling is a new digital bank', but at the time the high-street banks had put their content online (albeit in a limited way). The obvious retort from investors is: Haven't we already got digital banks?

Think in terms of the standout elements of the business, whether it is the size of the market, a novel use of tech, the strength of the management team, or the month-on-month growth rate to date. Don't assume that the investor will already know everything about the sector, and always avoid any jargon.

The problem being solved

State the reason why this business exists. Describe the pain point being solved, why it has been a problem and for how long. Summarize any user or market research that will back up these claims.

The challenge with this slide is, unless an investor has experienced the problem themselves, they often have a hard time accepting it is a problem at all. This means there needs to be an added layer here, describing the environment where this problem exists.

The solution

It is not enough to simply describe the solution – there also needs to be a nod to what it will replace. Think here of the famous Henry Ford saying: 'If I had asked people what they wanted, they would have said faster horses.' At the time, if he had pitched a car to VCs, they would have had no terms of reference. *What would people do with it? Where is the market?* There was an extra job to be done to show the horse and carriage market was firmly in Ford's sights.

If there is nothing yet to show, use a graphic representation of the solution, perhaps with screenshots of prototypes. The focus of the words that go with the illustration should be on the business benefits of the solution and what it *allows the customer to do*, rather than simply describing what the product does. Why is it compelling? Think in terms of saving people time, money or helping them in some other way, and how it will displace what is currently on offer. Again, include user and market research to illustrate the benefits.

The goal here is to explain the idea in *very* simple language, before going on to explain how big this idea could be.

A real game-changer in pitching is when there is a product to demo. If the product is complex or novel, it is very difficult for investors to understand what you are trying to do when you are trying to raise money off a PowerPoint. A demo shows exactly what you are trying to achieve.

The market

Here, there is a full description of the size of the total addressable market and any relevant sub-sectors, both from a historical perspective and in terms of projected future growth. Details should be included of current market share, together with a forecast of projected market share in the next three to five years.

In our case, our market centred around the 60 million current accounts in the UK, which at the time people rarely switched. Our goal, though, was not only to get people to switch, but also to open up a new trend where customers hold a number of accounts, thereby greatly increasing the size of the market. At this stage, though, with no frame of reference, it can be very difficult to explain how much the solution will disrupt what is on offer, but this is what you need to try to achieve.

This part will be important to investors, because there are lots of great ideas, but if it is such a niche proposition that the sales potential is tiny, the investment prospects won't be very enticing. Note, it is the *size* of the addressable market that should be highlighted. Investors always want to know how big this business can be at this stage, rather than how profitable. Profit is important, of course. However, no one knows the true numbers at this stage.

The tech

For some reason, investors always want the tech bit on one page, via some sort of neat infographic with all sorts of connected lines. With more complex products, this is not always possible, but start-ups need to do their best to comply.

Think in terms of describing in the simplest way what makes the technology so special, cutting edge and revolutionary. Include details of any intellectual property (IP), or regulatory considerations. If a highly regulated business, such as banking or pensions, include details of which ones apply and how in a separate slide on regulations.

The team

Introduce the team who will deliver this opportunity, highlighting relevant experience and achievements, whether in the sector or in previous early-stage start-ups. This can always be a bit of a minefield, because decisions need to be made about who to include and who to leave out and it can easily offend someone important on the team.

If any of the founders have worked together before, be sure to highlight this. Investors are looking for good chemistry.

When there is very little to show for the business, the experience of a founder becomes *very* important. Investors will want to know a lot more about their experience and their success with other projects/businesses. They will tie in what they hear here, with what a founder says they are going to do. Investors will ask themselves: do they believe that the founder can bridge the two?

For me, it is always a big bet on the founder. I'm focused on their track record and how their previous experience makes them the best person to be solving this problem. Then, I focus on the problem itself. How big a problem is it? Is it really real? Could this business fundamentally change things?

We will ask about the rest of the team, too, as well as the next hires. We like founders to share whether they have identified, say, a lead engineer, or a head of sales, who they will bring in once they get capital. We won't need to speak with these hires, though, unless they are absolutely critical to the business succeeding.

June Angelides, VC, Samos Investments

The operating model

The operating model describes how you are going to run the company and shows how the cost of delivering the unit will be less than the revenue from selling that unit. Over time, the gross profit will be more than the fixed cost and the business will make a profit.

Using solid calculations and research, describe how this business will make money. It can help to use graphics to explain the fee structure, unit economics and the interactions between different revenue streams.

Sales and marketing

There is always much discussion over whether the CEO is the person that does the selling. Obviously this is relevant in a business-to-business (B2B) market, where there will be a short list of people to speak to, but not entirely practical in a business-to-consumer (B2C) market, where there are potentially tens of thousands of customers.

Offer detailed plans of the customer acquisition strategy, including sales and marketing plans. Define customer acquisition costs and conversion rates and the results of any early test runs in the market that back these forecasts.

Competition

It is always a lot easier if there are at least two firms involved when trying to create a new market. It is a reassuring shorthand for investors that there is something to compete against, and a benchmark, rather than one business trying to create an entire market all by themselves.

List the key competitors in the market, and note evidence of any other start-ups looking to break into it too. Use graphics to illustrate key features of each one, strengths and weaknesses and points of differentiation. Saying there is no other competition, anywhere in the world, is simply not credible. There is always competition, even if the rival firms don't do it in quite the same way.

Financials

Read any blog or listen to any podcast on 'what investors want' and the vast majority prioritize financial performance. *The numbers*. They want to know about the market size, how much the start-up proposes to eat into that market and the pace it will do so. It is not just that they want data for the sake of data – they need to demonstrate the performance of the fund to other stakeholders. It is not enough to say 'Starling Bank looks great.' They need to back that statement with data.

Everything relevant must be noted, from a profit and loss forecast, to anticipated customer numbers, to churn, to gross margins. Include actual revenues to date, as well as a forecast five years into the future. Also highlight the forecast cash burn rate, and when the business is expected to become profitable.

> There can be the best idea ever, or the most up-to-date technology, but if nobody is willing to pay for it, then it won't scale. We need precise details on who is going to buy and how the business is going to make money. Is the pricing right and is the business going to make enough to cover all its costs? The commercial aspects of the business are crucial. If it doesn't add up, it is quite obvious.
>
> **Deepali Nangia, Partner, Female and Diverse Founders, Speedinvest**

Praise

Highlight key clients or contracts already signed, as well as any endorsements from well-known industry figures which will add weight to the pitch. If anyone ever said anything nice about Starling, ever, I was sure to note it. It gives the brand credibility.

The ask

Clearly define the amount being raised and what the funds will be used for, listing key milestones for the next 12–24 months. If applicable, list the prior funding history, noting how much has been raised to date and with whom.

Don't fall into the trap of trying to make this seem like an urgent, one-time offer. 'We can find space for you to put in £10 million but you'll need to act today because we're already committed elsewhere.' The investor will find out in due diligence whether it is an outright lie.

Conclusion

Create a memorable message by highlighting key points of the presentation. The goal is to make an impression and encourage the investor to take the next step. Think of a soundbite to stick in their heads and include contact details so they can get in touch.

> Ultimately, founders need to get to a position where the opportunity looks so great, it is a no-brainer for anyone but to invest in it. The way to do this is to be armed with data. The investors looking at a pitch may have never come across the sector before, or never invested in it, so if the data is there it will help them overcome their hesitation.
>
> Think about all the questions you might be asked, and the factors that might make any investors nervous, whether it is regulation, the size of the market or a significant competitor, and then come up with credible answers and rehearse them.
>
> **June Angelides, VC, Samos Investments**

Pitching dos and don'ts

Remember, aside from the initial contact to set up the meeting, this deck will be the first point of reference about the business. You'll want to present the concept in the very best light. Thus, in addition to the basic slide format, there are some additional dos and don'ts that will help give the pitch deck an edge.

Do tell a story

A good pitch is about creating a story. Yes, it is about the founder and what they are building, but storytelling will always capture the imagination. What is the magic you will deliver and why is it so engaging? It can help to describe users who have encountered specific problems that this product will solve.

The best stories about user needs are your own, or those of people you know personally, like friends or family.

All founders should get good at storytelling – it is one of the key skills every business leader needs. They'll need to call upon it to sell to investors, but they also need to tell a story to the team to keep them excited and anchored, so everything continues in the right direction. Then, they'll need to think of the story to tell customers to get them interested.

Do take care with the numbers

Specific numbers are good. They stick in people's heads. But don't bombard investors with numbers. There needs to be a balance. When talking about the business, the goal is to talk in numerical terms, rather than focusing on softer elements such as the culture of the company or the branding. However, peppering the deck with statistics can come across as too eager, almost desperate.

Aim to make any data visually appealing by creating charts and graphs. In fact, make sure the entire deck is visually appealing and the company branding runs through the presentation, using high-quality images and graphics. Needless to say, it should be carefully checked for accuracy, spelling and grammar.

Do prepare a pitch deck that can be adjusted for time

Investor meetings are booked into time slots, most of which are 10 to 20 minutes long, although meetings can be scheduled for longer. Prepare the pitch deck with enough flexibility so it can work well in any timeframe. Don't forget to allocate time at the end for questions and answers (Q&As).

Don't over-exaggerate

The challenge with writing any pitch deck is how upbeat to be. When selling the concept of Starling, I could have said *everybody* in the UK has a current account, so we have a potential market of 60 million account holders. If we went global, *everyone in the world* could have a Starling Bank account. *The addressable market is 3.8 billion people!* Was that realistic before we'd even launched, at a time when the UK's top six banking groups had a near-monopoly on current accounts and no one had even heard of a mobile-only current account? Probably not.

It would be a generalization to say that men tend to over-exaggerate while women tend to under-estimate in a situation like this, but this does often happen. It's a trait that goes back to prehistoric times. Men would return from the hunt and boast about the enormous bison that got away, or the giant fish they'd almost caught. They'd exaggerate to build up their status. The women sitting around the camp fire were focused on reassuring everyone that everything was going to be OK and took it in turns to fetch fruit and berries to make up for the lack of fish or bison. When raising money for high-growth business, it is the tall stories that win the day. *I will build the biggest company. I will send spaceships to Mars.* Women are more circumspect – *It will take me x number of years to reach these forecasts.*

Which is best? To under-promise and over-deliver, or the other way around? From an investor's viewpoint, there seems to be a preference for founders who over-promise. The problem then is it sets the entrepreneur up for a really bumpy ride. If it works out, they will be partnered with the investor for the next five years and will constantly be chasing their tail to live up to the over-optimistic boasts. Not to mention, if they have exaggerated the performance of the business, it leaves them wide open to the price being chipped once due diligence begins because they will be unable to produce evidence to support their wilder claims. I was always very realistic about what could be achieved and, if anything, played down any wild and fanciful projections. I prefer to under-promise and over-deliver. It makes it difficult to wow investors in the first place, but once you do, the journey is much smoother.

Don't include everything

This is not an information dump and, besides, investors don't have the time to trawl through a lengthy slide deck. The goal is to sell the big idea, which means filtering all the information available to prove this business has the edge. This includes not putting too much text on each individual slide. It will look messy and people will just skip over them.

Don't create bespoke pitch decks

It can be tempting to refine the deck for each investor, in a bid to give it an added boost. Your research may show that, say, this investor has recently put money into business B, which is in a complementary field, and you might decide to add in a line to draw useful parallels between your business and their recent investment. It's a nice idea, but impractical. For a start, you will be doing a lot of pitches. There's not enough time to continually edit and refine it to this level of detail for each one. There is also a danger that someone will forget to take the additional line out for the next pitch. Investors know that founders will be doing the rounds, but they don't want it rubbed in their faces by seeing a detail highlighted that was clearly directed at someone else.

Choosing your pitch team

Investors like to see a range of team members for the pitch, primarily the chief technology officer, chief marketing officer and, of course, the chief executive. There may be a temptation to build up the numbers to show off the impressive size of the organization, but founders need to be careful to only take people that know the script. Think, too, of how many from the investment side will be at the meeting. If they have indicated that only one person will be at the meeting, turning up mob-handed is not a good idea. Although, it is also wise to be prepared that these one-person meetings often inflate in size. I've been to plenty of investor presentations where other people wander in, sometimes halfway through the pitch, I assume because they have nothing else to do.

Give careful thought to how the presentation will be divvied up. In other words, who will say what and how long each person will speak. If the start-up is based on an equal division of shares among co-founders, it might seem like the fairest course of action to divide the meeting up on a similar basis. In some ways, it seems like a good idea, since investors dislike unbalanced teams. However, a rhythmic handover from one presenter to the next during a presentation can also be distracting. It is a better use of time when the more charismatic and extroverted members of the team do the bulk of the talking. They will inevitably be the best speakers. They can get over the 'everybody-is-equal' conundrum by lavishing praise on, say, the technical skills of the less-vocal founders. Then, later on, the tech person can make a *brief* presentation to add credibility to the whole pitch.

After meeting with more than 300 investors before finally securing initial funding for Starling, I met with a further 200 for further series of funding. As you might imagine, after hundreds of pitches, we honed our style. We knew the best team and who will say what and at which point. Even so, we were always open to improving our pitch technique, which is why, before one US investor roadshow, we brought in a specialist trainer to give us some tips on working together. After watching us give dummy presentations, one of his main conclusions was that the other members of the team were behaving too deferentially to me. In fact, he went on to ban them from looking at me before they spoke. There was even an instruction to talk over me occasionally. The goal was to give us a more equitable status, which would strengthen the pitch message overall. Whilst I can agree that it is important everyone plays to their strengths in a pitch, I couldn't help thinking a female coach wouldn't have been quite so quick to tell the rest of the team to interrupt the female CEO. That said, it is always good to keep checking a pitch to make sure everyone is on top of their game, so there was some value to the exercise.

Sometimes female founders are reluctant to bring in the experts to help them perform in these difficult environments and, in an ideal world, we wouldn't have to. But we need to give our best and succeed in putting forward our viewpoint. If anyone feels that they will be emotionally triggered by the dynamics in the room, or will get tongue-tied when challenged, it is best to prepare for it.

I worked with a business coach to improve my communication when I needed to navigate a particular investment committee. It was a very male environment and I expected some very robust questioning. I wanted to be able to come across in a positive way as I made the case for investment, but instinctively I felt I might not be my best self in that environment.

Coaches can pass on useful strategies to manage meetings better. For example, these pitches are inevitably quite data-orientated and investors want to be persuaded that you know the numbers in great detail. When presenting a summary of a 30-page pitch, one of the investors will pipe up and ask, say, the full year revenue projection for 2026. In that sort of environment, it can be very difficult to instantly recall those figures off the top of your head. Coaching will help you deal with it and push it back. You can say, 'That's a great question. I will revert after the end of this meeting with a full suite of numbers.' Just getting a feel for the style of language that is acceptable makes a real difference. It stops you standing there, looking like a rabbit caught in the headlights.

Check Warner, Co-Founder and Partner, Ada Ventures

Would I recommend a specialist pitch trainer to others? As with everything else with start-ups, if it is free, yes. There are some virtual pitch coaching sessions online, which offer free feedback and encourage founders to comment on the pitches of other founders. However, if you need to pay for it, probably not. Although, as above, it can be effective as part of a broader business coaching package. It is also worth noting that some investment funds invest in such coaching for the main principals running their investments because VCs recognize that running a fast-growing business can be a high-pressure, lonely environment and can take a real toll. Investing in coaching is in everyone's best interests. It can be really handy for founders when they come to future rounds.

I would, however, always bear in mind that the more people you speak with, the more they tend to give contradictory advice. There is no substitute for getting out there and seeing what investors think. They are the ones that count, after all. The most impactful way to hone your pitch style is to speak with real investors.

Whoever is included in the team, everyone should get together to practise the pitch ahead of the presentation. A lot. Going over the pitch together does help a huge amount. I would certainly want to be at the stage where everyone on the pitch team knows when to say their bit and to ensure that, while they are talking, everyone else on the team is smiling and supportive. The worst-case scenario is when people on the same side begin butting in, or glaring at one another, trying to steal each other's thunder. It does happen and, hardly surprisingly, it does not inspire investors.

Attend to the tech for online pitches

One final point on pitch preparation concerns technology. Today, not all pitches will be face-to-face. This has been a fantastic development for entrepreneurs trying to navigate a hectic round of investment meetings. Like most founders who have been successful in raising money, I've had my fair share of dashing over to the USA for a VC meeting that all parties subsequently realized was a waste of time within the first 10 minutes. Not only will the exercise have cost at least a few thousand pounds for travel and accommodation, but it would also have taken more than a day's worth of precious time. If founders have the energy, it is now possible to do a few pitches a day, in two different continents, online.

Aside from saving time and money, both hugely valuable commodities to founders, there are other bonuses here for the start-up world too. Video is much more controllable as a medium. While one person presents, others on the team can send messages to one another via Slack, adding relevant last-minute information to the pitch, or instant answers to tricky questions. From my own point of view, there is another positive, too. When I meet people face-to-face for the first time, they always seem a little taken aback by how short I am! No one can judge your height from a video, so this stops any initial awkwardness in its tracks. It is unfair, but meeting someone in person can open the way for unconscious bias. Online, investors can't so easily make judgements based on physical appearance. As one founder told me, 'It was so much easier to do the pitch via Zoom. No one knew I was pregnant because the camera only focused on me from the neck up.' Having a child is not a bar to successfully running a growing business but, as many female founders have discovered, some investors can't seem to get beyond that.

Thought does need to be given to the technology being used. Ideally, the system should have the capability to home in on the face of the speaker. There is nothing worse than watching a presentation given by a group where each person's face is nothing more than a pinprick size on the screen. It is impossible to know who is speaking and very distracting. Ensure too that the sound quality is top notch.

CHAPTER TEN

The pitch

Pitching well is an art. When you walk into that room, you need to be able to perform and put on a bit of a show to get people excited. This can be tough for those who are naturally introverted, but if you know your subject well (which you should do), you will be able to confidently present. This is something you want to bring into the world, so you are going to need to sell it. You need to demonstrate that you are a visionary: you know what this market needs. Plus, if you have done your homework as you should, you will be able to answer any questions well and easily assuage any concerns or reservations. At the end of the presentation, the goal is to leave everyone with the conviction that you are the expert in the subject matter being discussed.

I like unconventional products. One of my investments, Jude, is in the incontinence space, which is something that is traditionally taboo. Incontinence impacts a large proportion of the population who want to be active and involved, and participate in the workforce, but can't. I really liked Peony Li, the founder, when she came to pitch to us and found her incredibly brave. I couldn't see many men coming up with this business idea, let alone pitching it.

When I see big problems like this tackled, it really excites me. It was also inspiring to see the passion that Peony brought with it. She'd done her work, too. There was a ton of due diligence and she's spoken to so many people that suffer with it and recorded videos. There was so much to discuss. We just knew this wasn't someone who was going to change her mind in a day and do something else. She'd committed to solving the problem.

It's about execution, too. Did I believe she'd attract the best team, because you can't do this alone? Could this founder sitting in front of me sign up the best operators and the best tech people and sell this vision? Her pitch answered all of this.

June Angelides, VC, Samos Investments

My very first pitch was to the wrong firm, to the wrong person, about the wrong idea. I'd somehow managed to talk a large private equity firm into taking the meeting. This was the sort of business that invested £1 billion plus, at a time when I was looking for a few million at most, so there was zero chance they'd ever have invested. By the day of the appointment, the private equity contact had clearly come to his senses and sent his very junior associates to meet with me. Within minutes it was clear that they were dumbfounded by the idea of a new digital bank and had no understanding of how I was going to build one. To be fair, nor did I. I was fairly certain of the end result I was aiming for, but had zero sense of how to get there. I was completely new to the start-up scene and only had a vague notion about buying in the tech components I needed but, even then, wasn't certain of how I'd put them all together. Perhaps hardly surprisingly, the junior associates didn't know the right questions to ask me, to probe the concept further. Even if they had, I am not sure the answers I'd have given at that time would have been hugely helpful. Strangely, though, when I reflect on that meeting I realize that I intuitively knew at least some of the right answers. In fact, Starling Bank has become very similar to the vision I outlined at that meeting, the only significant difference being that it became four times the size of what I envisaged. One of the questions I was asked, for example, was why I had only made provision for 1,000 customer service staff. Established banks needed 30,000 people to manage customer queries, I was informed. I explained that the technology was going to be cutting-edge, therefore the customer experience was going to be excellent. There would be no need for so many people to handle queries and complaints.

My pitch fell on deaf ears. Back then, the idea of building technology like this from scratch was still hugely unusual and, as I said, I didn't explain it as well as I later learned to do. As any founder will discover, pitching well will involve a significant learning curve.

10 strategies to turn a pitch from 'OK' to 'outstanding'

There is a certain amount of protocol to an investor pitch, an accepted way that things are done. In most cases, the investor will kick off the presentation, spending two to three minutes talking about their firm, how they like to operate and the cheque size they write. Then it will be over to the founder to introduce themselves and the team they have alongside them that day. This is it: the moment when a founder and their team can either nail that pitch, or walk away empty-handed. With this in mind, I am going to share 10 strategies that I and my fellow female entrepreneurs have learned that make a real difference to the outcome of pitches.

1. The first 10 minutes count – a lot

A huge amount rests on the first 10 minutes of the meeting. This is where it becomes immediately obvious whether there is any mutual feeling of camaraderie in the room. When that connection is found, it is much easier to get across the main talking points without it feeling like a hugely formal presentation.

The very best meetings are the ones where the pitchers don't even get the deck out, and don't formally present the business. The environment is just right to talk it through on an informal basis. The detail can be discussed at the second meeting. Anyone that finds themselves being quickly ushered towards a formal presentation is in the midst of a bad meeting. The investor is going through the motions.

Long before I became a Dragon, I had a conversation with an investor about what he looked for when he spoke with entrepreneurs. His first criteria was to find entrepreneurs that he liked and could see himself spending some time with. He told me that sometimes he came across ideas he thought could really do well, but the person behind it was not his cup of tea. He knew he'd never be able to get behind it, because the people side didn't work.

The other elements he looked at, incidentally, were what sum he needed to get in and, crucially, when he could get out, and at what price.

Jenny Campbell, CEO, YourCash, and former Dragon

---

2. Get rid of the elephant in the room

Sadly, despite all the progress made, some investors will still turn up with preconceptions. The only way to turn this around is to remain confident and assertive. If you, as a founder, don't fully believe in the idea and your ability to deliver it successfully, no one else will.

> Something I learned when fundraising for Ada was there was an assumption among all-male investment groups that, as a woman, I would not be on top of the numbers. They had an unconscious bias that women could not be mathematically minded. I made sure that I pretty much only spoke about the numbers in the first two minutes of the pitch. I almost spelt it out. I'm incredibly *numeric*. I made sure they couldn't make that assumption.
>
> **Check Warner, Co-Founder and Partner, Ada Ventures**

3. Maintain eye contact

Once the introductions are over and the presentation switches to the slide deck, it's easy to lose any ground gained during the intro by focusing on the tech. There is nothing more off-putting that watching someone present their deck by effectively reading aloud what is on each slide. There is no added value at all. Maintain eye contact with the investors and talk in an engaging and direct way about the topic on each slide. And don't get involved in operating the tech. While the main person speaks, their colleague should operate the computer.

4. Think like an investor

When the nerves kick in, it can be easy to start waffling and talking for the sake of talking. If entrepreneurs focus on the wrong elements of their presentation, or are vague, or too expansive about irrelevant detail, they quickly lose a VC's attention. The goal here is to be concise. State the problem that's been identified, the solution and why this team is the one to make it happen. Don't waste time talking about all the things this business could one day turn into – just showcase what it can be right now, with the right level of investment.

Always remember that, while founders are fixated on the idea, investors think of terms of *markets*. Their thought process is: if there are X number of customers who'd pay an average of £y per year for what is on offer here, then the total addressable market is XX.

When it comes to pitches that don't go anywhere, what investors complain most about is:

- They don't understand the idea.
- They don't know how big the market is.
- They don't have confidence in the team that is trying to raise funds.
- They are not sure of the exact sum the start-up is trying to raise.

5. Cut the bull*@ (or technically known as BS)

Never try to seem more than you are. If you try too hard to seem corporate, or pretend to know things you don't, you will conceal your real talent. Investors are good BS detectors. Likewise, they are not impressed by jargon designed to show a deep knowledge of the technology sector, but which never quite hits the mark. The expressions on the faces of investors always cloud over when they hear an excessive amount about 'data mining', 'aggregation' and 'social networking'. Ditto if a founder uses unnecessary 'management speak', with expressions such as 'optimum levels' or 'tactical decisions'. It sounds ridiculous to hear a start-up speaking in phrases better suited to the pages of a FTSE100 company's annual report. Speak in language that is familiar and accessible to all. If you are new to an industry, minimize the risk of using terms incorrectly by staying away from technical terms.

Think also about the type of investor being spoken to. Institutions which invest in fintech and banks will understand terms such as 'return on tangible equity', while more consumer-orientated ones will be more interested in customer acquisition cost.

6. Don't stand in front of the bodies!

'Don't stand in front of the bodies' is an expression based on the famed *Columbo* TV crime drama. For some reason, the eponymous detective was forever coming across people who would guiltily stand in front of the key piece of evidence, or even bodies, in a bid to outwit him.

We tend to become fixated with issues that are important to us but are not that important in the whole scheme of things. If, say, there is an issue with customers unsubscribing after three weeks, the pitch team will talk extensively how there is *absolutely not* an issue with customers unsubscribing after three weeks. Why? Because we talk most about the things we worry about. However, by doing so, we only highlight issues to the investor that are not important to them.

7. Give clear answers to all questions

If founders lack confidence, they'll often try to dodge questions by fudging the answer. They'll mumble over the valuation, or sound apologetic, or even a little obstructive. This will get noticed and be marked down as a bad sign, which is not ideal in a situation when it is already hard to impress investors.

> I really value authenticity. I want to know why an entrepreneur is building what they're building and why they think they're the best people in the world to build this business. There is nothing that puts me off more than when I ask a question and they respond, 'Oh, I can't give you this information.'
>
> I looked at this deal in the luxury beauty space which seemed really interesting. The entrepreneur had created a sustainable alternative to a product that has mass appeal. I asked about the raw materials they were using but was told point-blank that they couldn't tell me this information because it was confidential. My response was: 'If you can't tell me this, how can I evaluate if enough raw material will be available for the numbers you are quoting?' There may have been an abundant supply at that time, but we needed to know there would be enough as the business grew.
>
> I wasn't planning to steal the idea. I just wanted to understand the business to make an informed investment decision. That is my job. I can't do it unless I have the full information.
>
> **Deepali Nangia, Partner, Female and Diverse Founders, Speedinvest**

8. Get to the demo quickly

If there is a prototype or a MVP, bring it out as quickly as possible during the pitch. This is real tangible evidence of how the product works and what the user experience is like, and it is a fast and effective way to get investors to engage.

9. Know your exits

If a start-up is seeking a large sum of investment capital, investors need to understand that there is a clear exit strategy. Is the plan for the business to go public, or is it planning to be acquired? Note, this exit strategy didn't feature in the suggested slides in the previous chapter. Exits are something investors ask about but are not a subject that founders should raise. VCs need to know that they can exit this business so that the VC can return funds to their own investors, e.g. the limited partners (LPs). Where it becomes tricky is they don't want founders to look too keen to get out and realize their gains because they need to be so fixated on the start-up that money doesn't matter. However, at the same time investors want founders to be able to voice a firm idea of how everyone will get their money out. It can be a bit of a tightrope to walk. Founders need to respond assertively to investor questions, but not look as though there are personally interested in this particular aspect of the proposal.

At this stage, it is too early to be entirely definitive about the proposed exit strategy, and definitely too soon to state authoritatively how much everyone is going to make out of the IPO or acquisition. However, all the good work preparing for this moment, and delivering a brilliant pitch will be wasted if the VC is privately wondering if they'll get their returns before they must return the money to their LPs.

10. Be honest – always

All entrepreneurs will try to paint a *very* rosy picture of their businesses. Investors expect this to a certain degree – it is part of the sales pitch. Founders will also most likely err on the side of inflating their forecasts because they don't yet know for certain how well the product will perform in the market. Again, this is understood, and these numbers will get tightened up as the process continues. But the positive outlook should not stray into the territory of lying or misrepresenting vital information. The potential outcome of this practice is a deal will unravel at a dizzying rate because any trust between entrepreneur and investor has been destroyed.

I've had a lot more deals accepted in the Den than have gone to fruition because a lot don't make it through due diligence. Various things happen. Sometimes the entrepreneurs themselves change their mind. On other occasions, the deal they've presented is not quite what is on offer. I shook hands on a deal with one woman to invest in a business making vegan ice cream. I'm not the world's biggest fan of vegan food, but this was lovely. I really liked the person, too.

When she pitched, she said she owned 30 per cent of the business, the rest of it was all owned by family and friends. I like my entrepreneurs to own more than 50 per cent of a business so they feel like it's their business. She told me that she had the option to buy them out 'at par'. In banking terms, at par means at the same price as they invested. I invested on that basis.

During due diligence, it turned out she didn't have 30 per cent. She and her husband owned 30 per cent, he had 20 per cent and she had 10 per cent. If she had walked into the Den and said she only had 10 per cent of the business, I would have said 'I'm out' straight away. Then, I discovered that family and friends don't want to sell at par either. That was the end of the deal. It was so frustrating.

Jenny Campbell, CEO, YourCash, and former Dragon

Post-pitch Q&As

Appointments with investors almost always end with time for questions from both sides. Though pitchers will have prepared thoroughly, they will never know quite what they are going to be asked, but they should prepare themselves for some tough questions. In fact, the tougher the better. It shows that the investor is engaged and interested in what they've seen. I've always said that the questions asked by Harald McPike, my first investor, were the toughest I had ever been asked either before or since. The setting for this three-day interrogation sounds impossibly glamorous, aboard his 92-foot yacht, *New Life*, sailing around the Bahamas. Harald (or Harry as he prefers to be known) had invited me there because he had become interested in digital banks and, after his people checked out the small group of neo banks looking for investors, had decided Starling was worth the once-over. I can say for certain that I could well have been anywhere in the world, as I didn't once get the chance to enjoy the view. I was too busy thinking on my feet, fielding a barrage of questions about every aspect of my business.

The approach was helped by the fact we had more time to speak than in a traditional pitch. This meant we had time to discuss how the banking industry was constructed and how Starling might fit into it. Thus, on the first day, we talked about the product and how Starling worked. On the second day we moved on to discussing the industry as a whole and the different ways banking might evolve in response to a digital bank like Starling. The next day, we moved on to analysing what needed to be done to produce the optimal product. While this sounds very structured, the conversation was not static. The subject matter went round and round, back and forth, up and down, as Harry asked about every aspect of the plan. It was intense, but what I enjoyed about it was that it brought my thinking forward. By the end of the time in the Bahamas, my thinking was different to how it had been when I arrived. I also passed muster with my answers, because Harry subsequently invested £48 million in three tranches.

It is possible that entrepreneurs won't know the answers to all the questions, particularly the toughest ones, and especially when they have previously only done one or two pitches to date. That is fine. In this case, the answer should be something along the lines of: I don't have this information to hand right this moment, but will send it over as soon as we get back to the office. This is a thousand times more preferable than a guess, or worse still making something up entirely on the hoof. Investors don't expect entrepreneurs to know all the details. Sometimes it is just as important to see how they react under pressure. It shows how adept they are at dealing with situations that may involve uncertainties.

Once again, female founders should prepare themselves for some degree of unconscious, or even overt, bias in the questioning. As detailed in Chapter 2, some female entrepreneurs report being asked by an (unenlightened) investor, 'What if you get pregnant?' The only way to cut through questions like this is to remain calm, answer truthfully and explain there would be a plan. No one is indispensable, whether male or female. People leave companies, or take leave, but as long as there is something in place to deal with the eventuality, it will not be detrimental. If the investor is not satisfied by this response, it is quite probable that they are not going to be the right investment partner anyway. If anyone feels uncomfortable with the way they are being treated, they should have the confidence to walk away.

Entrepreneurs should also come armed with their own questions, which have been prepared in advance. By the close of the meeting, the information that the pitch team should come away with should include:

- **Potential size of investment**
  Most funds will have an average size of cheque that they are prepared to write. Is it £1 million or £10 million?

- **Do they lead, or only follow?**
  Every investment round has a lead and then a number of VCs that follow. A lead investor will negotiate the terms and take, say, 30 per cent of the round, and everyone else will follow on from there. The problem is, few

investors want to lead. For two years solid, I found loads of VCs that wanted to follow, but not one wanted to lead. Again and again, I would hear: 'I love the idea – let us know once you have a lead.' Once there is a strong lead in place, all VCs want to follow. Getting a credible lead is always a huge step forward.

- **Primary and secondary**
  In most cases, VCs will make an initial investment, and reserve funds to maintain their stake in future rounds. This is usually in a ratio of four to one. Thus, if there is a £1 million investment in a seed round, a further £4 million is put in reserve for future rounds. The further payments are not a given, though, and will depend on how the relationship develops. It is worth ascertaining how often a VC does follow on with its other investments.

- **Does the investor typically take a seat on the board?**
  Not all VCs will expect a seat at the table, but a lot will. There are pros and cons to this, which we will go into in the next chapter.

- **Reporting requirements**
  Related to the above point, what are the investor's expectations regarding updates? Some expect quarterly updates, but it is not unheard of for VCs to demand a weekly report.

- **Due diligence**
  It's very useful to find out about how the process works should this go to the next stage. Every firm has a different way of proceeding, so ask about term sheets, access to financial and operational data, and how they deal with references and NDAs.

- **Competitive situations**
  What would happen if a competitor approached the VC to pitch? As I discovered, some VCs had no hesitation in sharing my pitch deck with a rival digital bank. I'm always keen to hear about their stated practice for sharing information within their portfolio.

Some of the answers you need may have been be covered in the investor's initial talk, and some of the questions about process can wait until the second, or even third meeting, once an investor has shown some interest. The lead-or-follow question should definitely be asked up front, though. If they are keen, but only keen to follow, the investment round is far from over.

In an ideal world, fear of missing out (FOMO) will take hold. The investor will sense the pitch is getting traction elsewhere and won't want to risk being the person who didn't spot the next Amazon or Meta. They'll move things forward, even if the product doesn't completely match their usual investment parameters. This is, however, quite rare.

The next best scenario, although also rare, is where a founder gets the pitch just right, their answers to all the questions are satisfactory and they succeed in communicating their passion for the business, together with their knowledge of the financials. Then, then they may, just may, succeed in making the investor as passionate about the business as they are. This is highly unlikely to happen on the first pitch to a VC, or the next one to a different VC, or the next one, or the next one, but entrepreneurs learn from each pitch they do. With perseverance and refinement, they may eventually find an investor talking about term sheets and the next stage. This will be an incredible milestone in the story of a high-growth business.

During the pitch, I am constantly asking myself whether I am really excited about this founder and what they are building. I listen hard to understand more about the background of the founders and why they've chosen to do this. I want to know about the size of the market and the competition, the churn rate and sales cycle.

I consider a pitch good if I leave the meeting and can think of little else for the rest of the day. It's a bit like going on a really amazing date. I'm already working out when we can meet the second time and whether or not they'll message me, or whether I should message them first.

Deepali Nangia, Partner, Female and Diverse Founders, Speedinvest

What to do when a pitch doesn't work out

When pitching to mostly male investors, it was hard work to sell the idea that women were happy to talk openly about pelvic floor health. One investor told me that women's health products were too 'niche', which seemed a bit odd since they impact more than 50 per cent of the population. If I made a mistake, it was early on, when I skirted around words like 'vagina', or anything else I thought might make male investors uncomfortable. I realized this wasn't helpful to anyone. After that, I devised the 'vagina test', basically seeing what happened when I introduced the V-word. It was fun and quite an acid test of whether or not we'd be a good fit for one another. The key then was to make sure I gave the best of what they wanted to hear: the numbers. What they need to know is the scale of the problem and the scale of the opportunity.

Female entrepreneurs do need a skin like a rhino. There's a fine balancing act between taking on feedback that is going to help your business grow and finding what to ignore or block out. People often give advice based on their own experiences, but that doesn't necessarily mean they are right. Women definitely get proportionately more negative feedback, with investors saying things like: 'You are not the right person to do this.' This is especially so in female-focus tech products. Male investors find it difficult to take them seriously. The only way to get through it and succeed is to have a laser focus on what you are trying to achieve.

Tania Boler, Founder, Elvie

Sometimes, it will become almost immediately obvious that you are not going to be successful and the meeting is not going well. It is always useful to remind yourself that there can be a range of reasons for this, over and above the fact that an investor doesn't really rate the product or service being pitched, or didn't gel with you as a founder. The VC partner may be about to deliver a paper to a conference on, say, advances in medtech, so takes a meeting with a few medtech start-ups to build up their sources of data on the market and save themselves time on researching their talk. For the investor, the meeting is purely about information gathering and they have no intention of investing in your venture. This happens a lot more often than you would imagine.

One of the most frustrating reasons that meetings don't work out is when the investor is already weighing up whether to invest in another, similar firm and is effectively benchmarking your start-up against the other one. If your business turns out to be the benchmark, the questions asked will always be clear indicators of this, as the investor will constantly steer the conversation around to the rival. I have had experience of this, and it is very disheartening and difficult to navigate. It was one of the very rare occasions where I met an investor alone, because something else was happening in the office that day which meant my usual pitch team were needed elsewhere. Right from the beginning of the meeting, though, it was clear it was not going to be about Starling and what we had to offer. I had launched into the pitch, talking about the bank and its progress, when the investor interrupted.

'What do you think about Revolut?' he said.

I politely answered the question about our digital banking rival by complimenting their business model and then quickly brought the conversation back to Starling.

'But how does the business model of Revolut work?' he pressed.

This time, I responded with a bit of a compare-and-contrast with Starling, figuring this could be an opportunity to talk up our superior tech.

'No, no, no,' the investor declared. 'I want you to give me a *good* answer.'

This was the first and only time I have called an investor out. This man was being overtly aggressive and he was wasting my time. It was clear he had no intention of investing in Starling and there was no way I was going to allow myself to be used as some sort of researcher for this firm. I had a bank to run.

The big question is, should female founders, indeed any founder, call out behaviour like this? There was a certain satisfaction about pushing back against this very unprofessional investor and the expression on the faces of his sidekicks was quite the sight. It was a big investment firm and the aggressive man was very senior. I'm fairly sure no one had called him out like this before. Yet, could speaking out be damaging in the long run? Many of the female founders I've spoken with have talked about being labelled 'difficult' when they stand up for themselves and this means they miss out on investment. (For the record, the investor in this story told me to my face that the firm would never, ever invest in Starling. This did not seem like a big loss, since they were clearly gearing up to invest elsewhere, although they didn't invest in Revolut after all that.)

After-meeting review

As a general rule, it is good to imagine a pitch is looking promising, right up until it is 100 per cent clear that it is not. Negative self-talk will affect your pitch, you'll be deflated and your energy will sap. It becomes hard to engage when this happens. Why push on when things don't seem to be going your way? Because experience shows that it is very easy to develop theories in your mind about how it is going, yet my own experience shows that most of my theories have been completely wrong. This is particularly so in any after-meeting review, where it is easy to convince yourself of one thing when the opposite is actually true. Signs you have misread the situation include:

- An investor is *hugely* enthusiastic and charming. It feels all-but-certain that they are ready to send over a term sheet, right? Wrong. They just didn't want a difficult and awkward meeting.

- The investor asks for another meeting to look at all the data. This has to be it, right? They're surely about to invest. But, not necessarily. You may have missed the signals during the meeting, but were they asking *a lot* of questions about your key competitor? If they were, that further meeting could be to mine your data to shore up their conviction to fund this rival. Your analysis will help them do their job.

- They tell you they have all their partners over from the USA the following week and ask if you would like to attend a formal dinner being held in their honour. 'We're inviting all the founders we are thinking of investing in,' you are told. This absolutely, definitely, has to be it! Except, when you go to the event, you'll take a look around and see you are the only woman in the room. Yup, you are that token woman. Your invitation is a bid to show that the firm is diverse.

- The investor finishes the meeting by mentioning that they are organizing a conference for leading VCs and asks if you'd like to speak on the panel. 'Since you are going to be a good friend of this company and we're going to do business together, it'll get things off to a good start,' they add, persuasively. As above, when you appear at the event, having spent valuable time preparing for your talk, you'll see that you are the only woman there.

If you read the signs wrong, and walk away from a pitch empty-handed, there is little that can be done than to pick yourself up and get ready for the next one. If you can, try to salvage something positive from it to make yourself feel better. There are learning opportunities even at the most unproductive meetings, and they can be used to refine the deck. Also, if another investor popped into the meeting, make a point of looking them up on LinkedIn. Find out who they are and what they are interested in. Then, next time you bump into them, have a conversation. Chance conversations like these often lead onto something else. Their firm wasn't interested, but they may put you in touch with a contact at another VC.

Above all, do what you need to do to stay resilient. Train yourself not to take criticism personally. When someone tells me that I have a really rotten idea, I immediately think that it is their loss. Since I'm competitive too, I use the rejection to my advantage. If anyone doesn't agree with me, I take it as a challenge to prove them wrong.

The other tool in my resilience armoury is humour. I've attended a fair share of bizarre meetings and it is really important to see the funny side. This is what will sustain you when things don't go as you'd like. Early on in the Starling investment journey, we tried our luck with family offices. We'd recently had a run of unproductive meetings with VC firms, so decided this option might be worth a go.

One particular family office was memorable for a few reasons. The first was that the office walls were made up of floor-to-ceiling fish tanks. It was hard not to be distracted by the super-colourful tropical fish gliding serenely past in the background as we spoke. Equally memorable was a mistake in the pitch by one of my colleagues who we'd chosen to demo the app.

'So, you just tap the app and you can tell you've bought baked beans at Tesco,' he declared confidently.

The rest of the Starling team shifted uncomfortably in their chairs. The app most definitely did not allow you to see a breakdown of what had been bought on the weekly shop. We had zero plans to introduce that level of consumer data in the future either. But, what were we to do? We couldn't stop our colleague in mid-flow and say he was talking rubbish. That would not be a good look in any pitch. But then we were presented with the worse possible scenario. The wealth advisor we were pitching to was very excited about the baked beans concept.

'Can you do cornflakes, too?' he asked, leaning forward in his chair, just as a clown fish passed behind him. 'And, if I weigh fruit, can I see how many kilogrammes of apples I have bought?'

To our horror, our colleague was nodding away enthusiastically.

'Would you be able to switch between pounds and kilogram measures?' the investor said, getting more and more engaged.

This was the moment we all came closest to breaking the golden rule of never, ever contradicting a colleague on the pitch team.

Negotiation

When a long series of investor 'No's finally turn into a 'Yes!' the next stage of the process starts with a term sheet outlining the basic terms and conditions of the investment. While this is a very exciting moment, any entrepreneur is advised to proceed with their eyes wide open and accept that not all term sheets go to a full investment. Lots of people will say that when term sheets are sent out, the deal is done. This is not so. The period between issuing a term sheet and the money hitting the bank is where both sides do their due diligence and things can still fall apart. The founder will appoint their lawyers and the investor will appoint theirs and acres of information will be passed back and forth. Both sides will be looking at everything on the way to dotting the i's and crossing the t's. Investors will need to be sure that the entrepreneur fully owns the company, as well as having the necessary IP, and that the books are accurate. They'll also look in minute detail at a whole host of factors most entrepreneurs may not even have considered. Meanwhile, founders need to be 100 per cent sure about what they are giving away in return for the cash injection outlined on the term sheet. It can sometimes be more than they bargained for.

Giving away more than 20 per cent of the company in an early round is too much. I know some VCs ask for 25 or 30 per cent equity but it's just not right. Founders need to project forward and think, okay, so they'll probably go through a few rounds of funding. Where does that leave them? A good VC will know that they need to keep a founder incentivized too, because they want them to be fully engaged in what happens next. Somewhere between 15 and 20 per cent is the right amount for the first round.

Sophie Adelman, Co-Founder, Multiverse and One Garden

It is only once both sides are satisfied with the term sheet that they can move on to working on the articles of association and shareholder agreement. The articles of association are a public document that will go to Companies House, detailing how the company will operate internally. This includes the different types of shares and procedures for issuing and transferring them, and the responsibilities and powers of directors. The shareholder agreement is an agreement between all the shareholders and the founders, outlining their obligations and responsibilities. This addresses what will happen to the shares if the founder leaves, as well as liquidity preferences, or anti-dilution measures, because if the company does go under, the investors will expect to get their money back first. There will also be a personal services contract, which is the founder's employment contract with the start-up. In each case, there will be a lot of discussion about what is in, and what's out.

What makes this a particularly tense time for founders is that the balance of power is very unequal. The investor has the money and the founder does not. Investor contracts are invariably written to be investor-friendly rather than founder friendly, which is why it is so crucial to get good legal advice at this stage. (We will cover this later in the chapter.) Ultimately, though, it is hard to put pressure on VCs when they hold the upper hand and, if the deal does fall apart, they have access to hundreds of other eager start-ups seeking investment. However, founders should never allow themselves to give away too much for too little.

You can, and indeed should, push back against terms that you don't want, but if you push back too hard, the investor can easily walk away. This happened to Starling with one of our first would-be investors, Route 66. At the beginning, Route 66 could not have been more enthusiastic about our partnership. The investor had quickly agreed to put in an initial sum of £3 million, followed by a further £10 million to £15 million over subsequent rounds. Equally promising for us, they were keen for a very swift resolution. This was great for two reasons. One, I had already used up all my savings and we were close to running out of money, and two, we were close to getting our banking licence. If we could secure investment, we'd be firmly on the path to launch, which would mean we'd finally get this amazing service into the hands of customers.

We'd already agreed the term sheet when, seemingly out of nowhere, the friendly, let's-get-this-done tone changed. Concerns were raised about what was owed to KPMG and PwC, which had continued to assist Starling on a contingent basis, putting their fees on the tab until we could afford to pay them. Route 66 demanded that we accepted a new valuation based on our debt obligations, dropping our £12 million pre-money valuation to £9 million. I pushed back. I had to. It was completely out of order. The deal abruptly fell apart and Route 66 walked away, only to subsequently inject more cash into our digital rival Tandem.

At the time, it was devastating. With the glorious benefit of hindsight though, I can see I was right to push back and, after a few further less-than-optimal events, Starling emerged better and stronger. I should also add, this is quite unusual. It's hard to get exact figures, but I am told that more than 90 per cent of term sheets do go on to become fully executed transactions.

The period of negotiation can be another point of vulnerability for female founders. Having overcome the challenges of securing funding, anecdotal evidence seems to show that male investors can be more aggressive in the deal-making stage.

There are some really bad actors out there that do prey on people that are naive and don't have any other offers from anywhere else. Female founders tend to be the ones with fewer options, so suffer most from getting those very unfair term sheets. Investors will charge a bunch of fees, or charge to sit on boards, or they'll take money out of the company and offer really aggressive terms. Most of all, the issue is on price. We know that female founders raise on average a third less than their counterparts and their valuations are lower.[1]

My advice to founders would be to be really smart about this stage and to gather as much information as they possibly can. This means talking to other founders who have raised recently, to better understand what they raised, and how much they gave away. Find out about the key terms that were put in their term sheet.

My other piece of advice is to invest in good lawyers. I'd never be afraid to spend money on really good lawyers because they're the ones that are going to go in and fight for you. That should all be paid for out of the fundraising round.

Check Warner, Co-Founder and Partner, Ada Ventures

While there have been moves by many VCs, particularly in the first round of funding, to make their term sheet as simple as possible, entrepreneurs do need to be sure of what they are signing themselves up to. Any mistakes now could become very costly down the line.

It is a good idea to find a lawyer you like working with now, because you will need lawyers at every round of fundraising. Subsequent investors will do extensive due diligence on your firm and will comb through all the contracts you have in place already to make sure everything is as expected. Likewise, you will need to do due diligence on the deal being offered. Appoint lawyers with a track record of dealing with VC investment, and it goes without saying that there is no obligation to sign up a lawyer on the recommendation of the VC you are in negotiation with.

I'm shocked by how many founders raise money and then delegate the legal detail to their team. These terms will impact you as an individual. This means you need to be all over them so you can easily understand them.

The thing that most people don't ever really seem to get their heads around is the preference stack. When a start-up is eventually sold, the money made is paid to shareholders in a predetermined order, the preference stack. As a rule, employees are last, while shareholders come first. As soon as entrepreneurs take venture capital money, they will want to have some kind of liquidation preference.

If the start-up succeeds, the entrepreneur will get on that treadmill of raising more and more VC money. The more they raise, the larger this preference class share is and the higher the risk that the founder might not be able to cash out. They become very much an inferior shareholder compared to investors.

It's very important to get a lawyer to make sure that you're well protected as a founder. Remember, also, every time you give something away, you've now set a precedent. Future investors will also expect that as a minimum. Most importantly, never give away more than 25 per cent to one shareholder, because at that point they will have taken control of your company.

Tania Boler, Founder, Elvie

Another area that founders should prioritize in this negotiation is their remuneration. As they will discover down the line, there is a reluctance to let founders take money out. In fact, the team in the layer below the founder often do better than those at the very top who originally came up with the idea and bear the bulk of the risk. The package received by those in the second tier tends to have considerably less scrutiny as they receive salaries and stock awards as a start-up progresses. The founder will invariably find themselves taking a lower salary to prove they have 'skin in the game' and may well not be the highest paid in the organization.

My own view is that it is not unreasonable that there should be a properly documented provision for any founder to take some money out after a few years. Investors would not expect founders to pursue the high life, but being able to live comfortably does not seem like much to ask, particularly when going through the high-pressure trajectory that is scaling a business. There needs to be some incentive and reward for this journey.

In negotiating the deal, founders should think about how they would like to be rewarded if everything goes as it should. They could include a clause that says if, say, the business achieves a £25 million turnover, they will be given some liquidity, or a pay review. If there is push back, the obvious retort is: wouldn't the investor be happy if the business reached that sort of income?

If this discussion is not had before the deal is done, it will become far more difficult to take money out of the business as time goes on. Investors are often very reluctant to let founders take any money out of a business, even when things are going very well. They may not say it directly, but there will be a subtle undercurrent to any such discussion that to do so is somehow greedy. It shows a lack of *commitment* to the business. It could be said that this highlights one of the disparities between investors and founders. Investors can sell their shares to release money whenever they wish, but the people actually running the business that is creating this wealth will often find themselves hard pushed to justify releasing any rewards for their efforts. To see off any future tensions, it is better to clear this up well in advance.

Working under pressure

The clock is ticking from the moment a term sheet is sent out. This is not just because the founder is desperate for a cash injection, having spent so long trying to find an investor while their early sources of funds drain away. Investors add to the pressure by imposing a period of exclusivity, barring founders from talking with any other investor while negotiations are going on. It is also not unusual for an investor to give company founders just 24 hours to accept the terms on the term sheet. Ridiculous as it sounds, it happens.

Exclusivity can be a bit of a trap. Once a founder signs the term sheet, which forbids discussions with any other VCs, it enables an investor to play hardball. They can extend the process of negotiation to pile on the pressure, and meanwhile the entrepreneur has the added peril of knowing that if they say a firm no and the deal falls apart, they will be starting again from scratch. Often, their financial situation is so poor, they just don't have that amount of time to 'waste'. Meanwhile, what makes the situation even more perilous is the amount of money spent on this process through lawyers and accountancy fees. Some investors offer abort fees, but it is rare and still more rare for them to actually pay out.

Just to add to it all, founders can even find themselves under a form of *collective* pressure. We talked earlier about lead investors and followers. Sometimes, it is the lead investor who recruits followers. They spot a good investment and then call in their mates from other investment houses who don't necessarily have a good deal flow (a pipeline of deals that comes to them). For the founder, the opportunity of a ready-made team of investment leads and followers might sound great on paper; it's a way to instantly complete a funding round. However, this close-knit group of investors can work together to further lean on a founder, encouraging them to agree to terms that are not necessarily in their best interests.

What entrepreneurs will find is that, as soon as they are sent the term sheet, investors will start hounding them to sign it. They'll *really* hound them. They'll call three times in a day asking, did you have any questions? What's going on? Entrepreneurs need to find a way to slow things down at this point, especially if they have previously spoken to another investor and are waiting for another term sheet. Obviously, it's not OK to go around shopping the first term sheet, sending a message saying, 'I've got a term sheet for X, can you improve on it?' But, if you were already in conversations elsewhere, there is a short window of opportunity. In all cases, it is really helpful to find ways to slow everything down and also decide (by taking references) if this is an investor you want to be working with for the next 10 years.

Sophie Adelman, Co-Founder, Multiverse and One Garden

The pressure to complete rapidly can come from the outside. too. Markets change, often very quickly. In a bull market, founders will have a bit more leverage in negotiations, but in a depressed market the investors call the shots. For this reason, it is a good idea to take note of the prevailing economic winds and adjust expectations accordingly. If the economy is heading towards a downturn, investors may not be as tolerant of any attempts to slow things down.

Things do get worse in a downturn. While most funds are well capitalized, there is a higher bar. There is a nervousness about investing in companies without clarification of how they will be capitalized further down the line. A lot of organizations will sit on capital to see which way the economy goes.

There are a lot of other mitigating factors, too. Right now, there is the war in the Ukraine, the growth in ChatGPT and Apple releasing upgrades that are making it more difficult and more expensive for founders to target their customers. Funds are not so willing to put a few million into a business and see how it goes.

In an environment like this, investors will be more drawn to the familiar. This can be a disadvantage for female founders, who may be developing businesses in areas that don't feel as comfortable or predictable to some investors.

June Angelides, VC, Samos Investments

The final bit of pressure will come from closer to home – the start-up team. They have bought into the vision and many will have taken a risk to join the company in the first place. Their futures depend upon the terms being accepted and the deal going through. Getting this close to realizing an injection of money represents is one of the most difficult moments for a founder. On the one hand, they are dealing with investors who are potentially playing hardball and, on the other, the hopes of the team rest on a successful outcome. I can still vividly remember how I felt each day when I walked into the office and saw everyone looking at me expectantly for news. They didn't need to vocalize what they were thinking. I knew. It was: *have you secured funding?* I found myself saying over and over 'We're nearly there. Don't worry, it's going to happen.' The personal pressure was immense.

Negotiation

What, then, can founders do to increase the odds of a favourable outcome? A result that works as much in the interests of the start-up as the investor. As with all negotiations, you must figure out what is really important for the other side as well as your own red lines.

Let's begin with the investor. This is where understanding how the process works really helps. The partner who heard the pitch might have been bowled over, but every investment has to be approved by their investment committee. All funds have strict fund rules about things they can or can't invest in and the terms they will agree to. These rules are solid and real and can't simply be negotiated away. There is nothing that can be done to change them. However, there will be at least some elements on the term sheet that have been set by the partner that fall outside these strict terms. *These* points are subject to negotiation. It is up to an entrepreneur to find out what these more flexible terms are and focus their efforts on asking for changes there. In other words, there's no point in going head-to-head and asking for something the VC can't give. You need to ask for things that they can give.

The way to find out what these negotiables and non-negotiables are is to do some leg work. Start with the partner and ask as many questions as you can. Then (if you have not done so already) do some research to find other founders who have taken cash from the VC and get in touch with them. Many won't have time to speak with you, but some might. Do accept though, even if they do have time to speak with you, there will be things they can't say because of confidentiality obligations. Another possible source of information is your legal team. Very often, lawyers familiar with the start-up community with have experience of certain VCs and have knowledge about their red lines.

> Getting another founder to look at the terms gives you advice you can really trust. Lawyers will be able to tell you what the terms mean and to advise you commercially on whether or not they make sense. But, another founder will also be able to tell you whether those these terms are fair. There are definitely terms to watch out for.
>
> Negotiating is hard, but I always say to work out which thing really matter. Don't negotiate on every single point. Just find the ones that are going to be meaningful to you, or harmful, and negotiate on them.
>
> **Sophie Adelman, Co-Founder, Multiverse and One Garden**

In an ideal world, negotiation should be a dialogue back and forth. Founders should be prepared to fully explain *why* something is not possible right at this moment. Say, for example, the investor is insisting on a seat on the board. In this scenario, it is a red line for a founder and their research shows that this is something the VC might give way on.

In which case, the founder might say, 'We don't need a board yet. When we do, we want to first take time to really understand who can add value to the business.' After all, when someone does sit on the board, they will be making very big decisions about the start-up. If progress can't be fully made on this term, try to insist that, in the paperwork, the founding team has the option to remove an investor from the board under certain circumstances, such as if they are being detrimental to the business.

Even if it feels like you are getting nowhere in your efforts to get some terms changed, it is crucial to remain calm, be patient and focus on those red lines.

If you are head-to-head with somebody and they have a negative emotive response to you, you tend to notice it quite quickly. People like this just don't like it when you push back. If you mirror their behaviour and they don't respond well to it, and then it is clear they don't want an adult-to-adult relationship. In a case like this, there may need to be a bit more of a staggered approach to negotiation, otherwise you are in danger of wasting a lot of energy and even creating more problems.

A staggered approach is where you take a step back and deal with the negotiation in a different way; I will give you my information and you give me yours. The discussions will go backwards and forwards in that way, rather than negotiating in the moment. If you try to negotiate in the moment with people who are behaving in a hostile way, all the baggage gets in the way of the actual logic of discussion. They'll be too focused on the emotional side and thinking about how you are challenging them. Their ego will get in the way of the negotiation and your focus will move towards managing their ego more than anything else. You won't really be in control of the negotiation anymore.

Zandra Moore, Founder and CEO, Panintelligence

Walking away

Investors think I am extremely difficult because I negotiate hard and take it to the wire. A founder has so much more skin in the game than the investor and will spend more time thinking through the negotiating strategy to make sure that the important points are won and the investor wins the 'nice to haves'. But, if both parties think they have won then that is a nice outcome and is much better than either party believing that they've left too much on the table. Most importantly, I am prepared to walk away if the term sheet, or more typically if the term sheet when translated into the documents, is just too unfavourable.

It is extremely rare for founders to walk away, but if every single one of their red lines is crossed, it might be the right option. If they move forward with a bad deal, it will have a detrimental impact on the business all the way down the line, well into the future.

Founders are so happy to finally be getting in some money, that they sometimes don't properly register what they are signing up for. When I've seen a founder about to sign a terrible term sheet, I will say, 'Look, I know this looks amazing and seems to solve a lot of your problems right now, but trust me when I say you will be creating more problems for yourself in the future. There are just some awful terms in that term sheet.'

We see this especially when the economy is in a downwards cycle, and investors use it as an opportunity to get more for less. It's important that founders realize that this economic climate is not permanent. If they sign up, when things do start to get better they will be in a very contentious situation where their business might, at the whim of an investor, be changed, and there's very little they can do about it.

It's not just a short-term issue, either. A poor deal will have a negative influence on further rounds of investment. A seasoned investor will look at the previous deal and note that the founder has so little equity there will be no skin in the game for further investors. Not only that, but they will perceive that there is little to incentivize the founders. Why would this entrepreneur put their complete energy into the venture when they get barely any benefit? I have seen further investors walk away from businesses like this, even when there is real evidence that it is performing well.

Future investment funds will also question the founder's judgement, wondering why they let the individual investor in on such terrible terms. Knowing that the first investors are bad actors will also deter them from coming in, because they won't want to be in a situation of working alongside them. Grabbing a poor first deal because it was the only one on the table will cause problems in the long run.

June Angelides, VC, Samos Investments

Whatever happens, founders should accept this process is going to be incredibly stressful, they are going to have to concede on some points and they are going to have a few sleepless nights. When all is said and done, if they make some progress on their negotiations, they may take the decision that this is the best offer they are going to get. As long as they have covered the basics, and the deal is not detrimental to the business or themselves, they may take the offer on the table.

Ultimately, when you take capital from an investor, you will be giving away some control, no matter what. You have to be pragmatic at a time like this. Life is not perfect and it is unlikely that any pitch will end with the founder getting everything they asked for. It might be better to look at it from another angle. You've been pitching for a long time and this is the best offer you have. If you don't take it, it will disappear and you'll be back to square one.

Deepali Nangia, Partner, Female and Diverse Founders, Speedinvest

Note

[1] L Halilou. Investors require more education on solutions for women, Docsend, 30 May 2023. www.docsend.com/blog/investors-require-more-education-on-solutions-for-women (archived at https://perma.cc/ZHD2-WZU5)

CHAPTER TWELVE

Investor relations

Everybody thinks when they take outside investment that they are trading money for equity. That's not it. They are trading money for *control*. Every time you give away a bit of your company, you are lessening your control over your company situation and your own personal situation.

Alex Depledge, Founder and CEO, Resi

I can still vividly remember when the investment of my first funding round landed. I moved from a state of being terrified of not being able to raise any money, to being terrified of losing it. Not losing it by failing to live up to my pitch. I mean genuinely losing it. Gaining funding meant that I went from being in debt, to a position of having £3 million in the bank. Some ex-Starling people were still signatories on the account. It was an oversight, but while I hadn't needed to think about that before because there was nothing in the account, I did then. I was so nervous that I called our then bank, Lloyds, and kept calling until I managed to speak to someone that was prepared to resolve the situation there and then. I remember it was Christmas Eve and it was the most important thing I had to do before the holiday. Receiving the money is, of course, just the start of the investor journey. While it might be tempting to celebrate (and, of course, you should celebrate each milestone, especially one this significant), there are other implications to be considered.

Life for any start-up in this position is about to become very different. Think about it this way. During the negotiation, there will have been ups and downs, but both sides were courting one another so everyone was for the most part on best behaviour. They wanted the deal to happen. Once the deal is signed, both sides will celebrate having found a common interest and look forward to sharing a rosy vision of the future together. Now, though, when the job of realizing the promises made at that pitch begins, everyone will begin to show their true colours.

My original deal to buy Hanco ATM Systems out of RBS was going to be backed by private equity, but they pulled the plug on me at the eleventh hour. I ended up with three or four high net worth investors. One month after the deal was done, one of the investors called me and said they'd like to review the business plan. The original plan was all about scaling the business by reinvesting revenue. He announced they did not want to do that anymore and they wanted to sell their share. Bearing in mind they had 65 per cent of the business and the management team had 35 per cent, it could have been really painful.

I could have gone toe-to-toe with him in the board meeting, shouting the odds that this wasn't what we agreed. It was difficult not to, because the news was a bolt from the blue. I stayed calm and went back two weeks later to lay my cards on the table. I told the investor that if that is what they wanted to do, the management team would sell their stake too. He was really surprised and said we couldn't do that because we were part of the business.

'We need you guys in there to sell the business,' he said.

My response was that, in that case, we were agreed. We would stay to grow the company and work together to find an exit for the investor in a few years' time, as originally agreed.

I faced the investor down, but in a controlled way. I'm pretty sure if it had been an all-male board versus this investor there would have been a boardroom battle and everyone would have ended up with nothing.

Jenny Campbell, CEO, YourCash, and former Dragon

Like any relationship, it will need working at right from the start. This is especially so if there is any mismatch in expectations. An inexperienced founder might *think* no one from the VC is likely to turn up for six months or so, to give things time to bed down, whereas the investor might want to send someone in from day one 'to help'. Likewise, the founder may have agreed that a representative of the investor has observer rights in board meetings, or even a say in proceedings via director rights. At this stage though, they have no idea how their new partners are going to utilize these rights, or how intensively they intend to become involved.

Aside from the uncertainty about how everything will settle down, there will be a new face, or even a bunch of new faces, for the start-up team to get used to. What many entrepreneurs don't realize is that when they sign with an investor, many of the people who turn up at the office the Monday morning after the money hits their bank account may not be the ones they actually negotiated the deal with. In addition to the partner who gave the nod to the pitch, another person VCs may send in is known as an operating partner. Operating partners are often a little older than the partners that founders have dealt with thus far, and more experienced when it comes to the day-to-day running of start-ups. They may even come from a background as a successful entrepreneur themselves. Equally, founders may find themselves being introduced to observers who know very little about running a start-up, or even someone who is a quite junior associate in the VC organization.

The first reaction (and one best kept private) is: 'I didn't sign up for this. I always gave the required answer when investors asked me the question, what do you want from an investor? I told them I wanted access to new markets and expert operational experience. In reality, my number one need was money!' But, of course, you did sign up for exactly this.

And never lose sight of the fact that there is a plus side to bringing in this partner. A plus side over and above the purely financial input. When a start-up signs with an investor, there is now someone to share the burden with, someone who has a real financial stake in the business, and who is aligned with the founder and management team. They will feel the pain if something goes wrong. The pain will not be as intense as the founder's pain, but it will nevertheless be felt. Plus, the VC and the operating partner they assign to work with each start-up do have real, valuable experience that they can share, which can be very advantageous to a high-growth business.

Investment has changed a lot over the past 10 years. Early on, the perception was that the private equity value-add for investors was all based on financial engineering. But that is just one tool in the private equity toolbox. Venture capitalists and private equity managers need to be able to work intensively with the companies in their portfolio, which in turn opens a lot of opportunities for entrepreneurs. Experienced investors attach experienced teams to their portfolio companies who can help with everything from marketing to talent management. They are not solely interested in the financial side – they also want to provide input on the business plan and help the enterprise deliver on it.

Helen Steers, Partner, Pantheon

It is inevitable that the perspectives of both parties will change over time as the business evolves and scales. On occasion, those perspectives won't be as aligned as they once were. The reality is, if you have accepted investment, you will be working together for a minimum of five years. Sometimes longer, or sometimes shorter, depending upon the way that the business progresses and the exit possibilities. You will need to find a way to work together during this period. Founders must be prepared that at least a proportion of their time will be spent on keeping their investor happy.

How to work effectively with an investor

First and foremost, the key to any successful investor/founder relationship is when the start-up delivers on the promises made at the pitch. It is almost certain that some sort of reporting system to relay progress will be built into the contract, but it is crucial that the start-up sticks to it. Generally, the larger the sum invested, the more regular the reported updates need to be. Starling Bank has always shared weekly updates with its largest investor. These updates are hugely detailed, too, showing customer numbers, a breakdown of the different sorts of customers, details on the balance of deposits, revenue and costs. The monthly pack we share with investors is even more detailed, running to 600 pages.

For anyone who is thinking this seems like quite the commitment, look at it from the other side. Would you lend someone £1 million, £5 million or even £40 million of your own money and not want to know how things are going? Plus, don't forget, it is highly likely that you will be returning to this investor at some point to ask for more money. You need them to be enthusiastic about the prospects for further growth. That enthusiasm comes out of regular communication.

Getting together all the stats about the business that investors require should not be too onerous a job. This is information that any high-growth business needs anyway in order to run effectively. Indeed, for companies that are highly regulated, such as those in financial services, there's a legal requirement for a great deal of the information to be on hand anyhow. This is a good opportunity for those in other sectors to get into the habit of meticulous record keeping too.

Something that won't come easy at first is reporting bad news. However, full transparency is key to a good investor relationship. What investors really hate is when their partners repeatedly say they are delivering, when in reality there is no discernible sign of growth. They believed enough in a business to invest, but they have responsibilities to their investment funds too and need to share credible data.

> One of the things we learned quickly was to send regular updates to investors to let them know what was going on. It was difficult sometimes, because not every quarter was a great quarter but, when you maintain that discipline and reliability, it shows you are a good steward of investors' money. Many of our investors have said this was a contributing factor to them investing again.
>
> **Romi Savova, Founder and CEO, PensionBee**

Over-promising is one thing, but not being able to show any progress at all is alarming for investors. Even more so than that, lying is just criminal, full stop. The standards of behaviour required for a director of any company are extremely high and especially so if they have accepted investment. Founders must be totally upfront and honest, even when milestones are missed, because they have fiduciary duties. Failing to inform investors when things are not going as expected will breach any undertakings made in the investment agreement.

> Once I make an investment, I am building a relationship with the founder. I want them to be open and honest with me and tell me the good, the bad and the ugly about their business. I want *all* the data. In return, I am very supportive and will offer advice and relevant contacts where necessary. I will speak to them regularly, every day in some cases, and even wake up thinking about their businesses in the early hours.
>
> **Deepali Nangia, Partner, Female and Diverse Founders, Speedinvest**

Another time when it is especially important to consult with investors is when there is any possibility that the start-up might deviate from the plan. The roll-out that was funded by the investment round might prompt a rethink once more customers trial the product. Even if this simply involves a small tweak, this must be in partnership with investors, with them kept fully informed all the way. If the change is an entire pivot, this is even more so. The founder sold them the big idea and, if it doesn't quite work as billed, they will need to sell them the replacement big idea. A pivot can provoke a delicate balancing act for any founder. It is unwise to completely rubbish the original concept, which they were once so passionate about. That would lead to a loss of credibility. The investor may also have strong views on how far they will allow a business to pivot.

How much power does an investor wield?

As founders will soon discover, VCs tend to work at a number of levels. They will provide useful commentary on the industry, sector and economy. Entrepreneurs can expect to receive occasional notes that are distributed around the investor's whole portfolio giving general market updates. They'll say something like: 'We're on the brink of a downturn, there is no further money to be raised, keep an eye on your costs.' Or, they will invite their investments to a seminar on the latest in AI, or to a wellness retreat for exhausted and stressed out founders.

Then, there is the more direct, hands-on approach and this is where start-up teams need to be quite thoughtful in their response. VCs will often ask companies in their portfolio to do tasks outside of the very important work of scaling their business. Founders may find themselves facing requests such as:

> 'My brother-in-law is in technology and is looking for a job – can you meet him?'

> 'We've also invested £100,000 in a company that does corporate away days – do you want to book a team-bonding session?'

> 'We're putting together a workshop to evaluate company G for a possible investment – can you come along to take a look?'

The most important asset any entrepreneur has is their time. We need to focus it and protect it at all costs. I know I have annoyed my investors in the past by not buying from their other portfolio companies, or attending seminars. But I am unapologetic about it. Founders need to be disciplined and say no, and keep on saying no.

> There are times when VC connections are very useful, but if you are not careful you can spend your whole time just meeting connections. I see a lot of founders out for coffee all the time and think: *you need to close that down.* If founders find themselves being asked to meet connections, they need to be able to say 'No, we have certain timelines. Let me come back to you on this in a couple of months.'
>
> **Tania Boler, Founder, Elvie**

And so to the closer, seemingly more relevant day-to-day interaction with investors. As I said at the outset, operational partners do, frequently, have some valuable intelligence to add to the mix, particularly those who have built a high-growth business in the past. However, this is not *always* the case. Now and again, operational partners put forward ideas that can be, how do I put this politely, completely irrelevant. I'll give you an example of one of Starling's investment partnerships. In this instance, the investor's operational partner had observer status on the Starling board. One day, this observer decided to take his role one stage further with a suggestion. Why didn't I print my personal mobile number on all Starling debit cards?

'If there are any problems, they can get in touch with you direct,' he said.

At the time, the number of Starling cards on the market numbered in their thousands, not in the millions as they do today. Even so, I had to tell him that I didn't think it was possible. Apart from the security issues, it just wasn't a scalable concept. He wasn't to be put off, explaining that another investment he'd worked with, a restaurant group, featured the name and contact details of the CEO on the wall. Thus, if the customers had any issues with their meal, they could go straight to the top.

'How many restaurants in the group?' I pressed.

It turned out that the restaurant 'group' comprised of just one outlet. This made this proposition a world away from a bank handling thousands and thousands of transactions every 24 hours.

How do you handle a situation like this? The problem is, you have taken their money. It would be unwise to say something along the lines of 'This idea is risible.' Investors have so much influence over your firm and it is important to keep the relationship positive. My tried-and-tested strategy is to wait for a good idea to come along and be hugely enthusiastic about that. I am non-committal but not rude about all of the less-than-optimal ideas that were put forward before it, but I really go to town when something might be viable.

A polite, yet firm, form of words needs to be found to say the equivalent of 'The purpose of an investor is to challenge – not to give the answers.' If you believe you know the answer, stick to your guns. All being well, they will lose interest on pushing the point. VCs can't force a founder to do anything. If they really, really want something done and a founder won't do it, then they will need to force them out. That is clearly the nuclear option that is in no one's interests.

If founders find themselves in a position where an investor becomes insistent on a possible course of action that they feel is impractical, they should remind themselves that they know their start-up better than anyone. The investor will be dealing with 10 or 20 other companies, while founders have been laser-focused on running their own business. Founders should have a greater insight into what is right or wrong, or just not feasible. No one understands a business as well as a founder.

Sadly, female founders will still find themselves being labelled as 'too emotional' or 'aggressive' when others want to push a point. In this case, it can be better to keep quiet and simply go away and come back with the answer. Over time, though, this can be an increasingly difficult position to take. One female founder relates a story of ongoing tensions with an investor. He was pushing hard for certain strategies, which she didn't feel were a good fit for the business, or the market they were targeting. Eventually, after several weeks of backwards and forwards, the investor exploded with rage.

'You don't listen,' he said. 'You never listen. I need to speak to your husband to find out whether you listen to him.'

Needless to say, the relationship soured after that. The investor was persuaded to back off a little, but has since spoken to others claiming the founder 'has a problem with men'.

These stories are regrettably more common than most people think. Unfortunately, they are rarely spoken about. Women who do speak out are branded 'troublesome' for not toeing the line, or dismissed as 'a radical bra-burning feminist'. (And yes, this happened to one of the founders we spoke with.) Oddly, though, if you look at these 'forthright' women they seem to get along just fine with senior male members of their own team.

The most successful way to navigate any tension is to listen, listen, listen and say you will come back to them. There is nothing that says you need to respond in the moment to their opinion, or any idea they are pushing strongly in your direction. You can go away, do your research, consult the data and have the conversation with whoever you need to speak with. Just by allowing this space, you will be able to come back with a considered response. It keeps the emotion out of it.

Women often feel they need to respond immediately, or to comply with an instruction. We don't. And we shouldn't have to. Just say confidently, 'I will come back to you on that.' That way, you will control the narrative.

If you can't find a sensible dialogue with the main contact, it might be a good idea to speak with one of their peers, such as another partner in the organization, to say, this is not helping. It is actually creating problems and more friction. It is not in anyone's interest for this to happen.

Zandra Moore, Founder and CEO, Panintelligence

What to do if it doesn't work out

It will feel like hard work at times, but good investor relations are crucial to the success of a high-growth business and future funding rounds. No business wants to be in the position of being the start-up that is quietly dropped by an investor because it did not meet expectations. To remind you of the VC model, out of 10 investments, only one will be the true star and maybe two or three will just about make back the original stake. The rest will almost certainly fail. Clearly, any founder wants their business to be that star.

If you ever want a clue as to where an investor thinks your venture sits on the VC equivalent of *Hunger Games,* look at the seniority of the operating partners involved in the business. If the operating partners become more and more senior, that is a good sign. The investor clearly believes this business has the chance to give them the coveted 10x return. If, on the other hand, operating partners are swapped for ones that are more and more junior, well, it is pretty obvious where the investor thinks things are heading.

For a while, the junior associates will seem very excited about the whole thing and be willing to get stuck in, even when things are going badly. However, when the older, more experienced operating partners run for the hills, it is always a terrible sign. They want to be as far away as possible from a failed start-up.

Ultimately, there will be a number of possible endings for any high-growth businesses. The most preferable is, of course, that it soars ahead, realizing all those carefully laid plans made at the beginning of the process. Maybe even exceeding them. A little less optimal, but not a disaster by any means, is an early exit. This is where the business is sold a year or two after launch to a trade buyer or a competitor. The founder will get their money out of the business and, all being well, a little on top. Many favour this type of exit, because it also means that their teams keep their jobs and are properly looked after. These sorts of deals usually come with an earn out clause, where the founder will receive a down payment, and then the rest comes after hitting certain targets further down the line. On a similar vein to the trade sale is an 'acqui-hire'. This is where a business buys a start-up with the specific aim of recruiting the team. The original product everyone spent so much time developing may never see the light of day, but at least everyone is in work. They may even be retained on much better contract terms. The worst-case scenario is that the company folds. Like so many start-ups, it runs out of cash and does not stay the course.

If a start-up doesn't make it, the tradition is for the founder to write a letter to Medium, the online entrepreneurship publication. The idea is to detail what was learned and it is said to be quite cathartic. The big question is: what next? In America, it's quite normal to climb back onto the horse after a few months and begin another start-up. For some reason, this doesn't happen so often in the UK. That is a bit of a shame. We learn so much on the start-up journey, it would be a waste to never ever consider an entrepreneurial venture again. It is quite possible the second one will succeed. Tough though it may seem at first, anyone who loses their first start-up should embrace failure and move forward. And, here is the thing, if you never try, you will never know.

CHAPTER THIRTEEN

Further investment rounds

There are two schools of thought when it comes to fundraising for high-growth businesses. Some say that any start-up should be *permanently* fundraising. They will argue that it is difficult to get investment, so it is wise to build relationships with investors even when there's no pressing need for additional money. Plus, it is easier to build solid relationships when the power dynamic that is usually involved with pitching is not ever-present (this is the mismatched dynamic mentioned earlier, where the investor has money, and the founder has none). Others will insist that endlessly trawling around VCs is a complete waste of time. Why schmooze investors when there is no need for additional capital? It is far better to spend time working on scaling the business. Occasionally, the same person will tell you both things. I was told in one meeting not to waste my time going to talk with investors when I didn't need to at that point. Then, just minutes later, the person in question informed me that the best time to speak with investors is when you don't need any money.

My own experience didn't quite fit into either camp. Starling's first fundraise was completed at the end of 2015, but could have been seen as much more than an A series round. As agreed during the initial discussion, Harold McPike followed his initial £3 million investment, with a further one of £15 million and then £30 million once the bank met previously agreed milestones. Although we had spoken with many investors in the interim, we didn't start our next fundraising round in earnest until early 2019.

As a general rule, series A funding is used by start-ups to develop their offer, refine the business model and establish market share, while series B is all about taking the business to the next level so it can begin to scale the opportunity. Series B funds are used by start-ups to meet the costs associated with high growth, such as business development, marketing and expanding the team, all elements required to reach a much wider market. By the time a start-up reaches series C, it is highly likely it is now showing signs of becoming a serious player in the market and is enjoying a good degree of success. Series C investments may be used to develop new products, break into new markets, or even to begin acquiring other businesses to expand the offer. As a start-up scales, it becomes less risky so, by series C, founders may find more sources of funds available to them via hedge funds, private equity firms and traditional fund managers who will feel more comfortable to get involved now there is evidence of a solid financial history.

There is, of course, still the option of growing organically, reinvesting revenue into the business. This can be a very successful strategy, as Sam Smith shows, but this means a start-up will scale at a much slower pace.

It took me 10 years to build my business to £2 million turnover. These were 10 very hard, very slow years. We didn't raise any capital, instead reinvesting income back into the business. When you reach critical mass, doubling turnover takes the same amount of effort as building it to that stage. Once you've doubled it to £4 million, then the next doubling takes you to £8 million and then it is £16 million. Scaling is not as hard.

I also found it helped to think of the next target in line. When the next goal was £8 million, I was already thinking of £16 million. When we got to £50 million, I was already thinking ahead to £200 million. My own personal big picture had to be bigger than the target. I set the team bigger targets too. When you change your mindset to think like that, it opens up the window to that opportunity.

Sam Smith, Founder, finnCap

For many founders, the idea of being in permanent fundraising mode will make their blood run cold, especially if their first experience was particularly challenging. The process for subsequent rounds is, however, different. It is not like starting from scratch.

Series B fundraising usually begins once a start-up has passed a number of milestones. Since it is more established and the business model has advanced, it will attract a higher valuation. Investors will pay a higher price for equity, but the associated risk will be lower because the start-up has shown that the product works and is in demand. There will also be a lot more information available about the start-up's track record, the abilities of the management team and how effectively it used the money from the previous round.

During the first round of funding, the A series round, VCs will usually inform entrepreneurs that they have put aside funding for further rounds. They do this because they need to protect their stake in these subsequent rounds. Say, for example, a VC invested £10 million to get a 20 per cent stake in a start-up in the initial round. If they don't follow the money by taking their proportion in the next round, the VC's overall percentage share will decline. However, the A series round VC will not usually want to lead the B series round, because a new investor is needed to push up the value of their share in their fund. The value of that £10 million stake stays at £10 million until a new price is set. The new series B investor will lead the round and set the price, which is how the £10 million stake can become worth £20 million. They would most likely bring in further new investors to follow, and then the series A investors would top up their investment. Thus, the first investors would maintain their share, but have fewer shares this round for a larger cost to them.

From the founder's viewpoint, it is good to bring in entirely new investors too. Aside from the fact it pushes up the valuation, it extends their connections. Close ties with a range of investors means more funds to speak with when additional money is needed. And high-growth businesses *always* need more money because scaling burns through capital. On the plus side, when valuations go up, founders give away less equity for more money. However, what founders do need to understand though is, with each successive round, investors will be coming in above them in the preference stack. If a company raises £100 million in successive rounds, but is later sold for £80 million, VCs will share that figure, with the most recent investors getting the largest share. The founder would receive nothing in this scenario.

The same, but different

All funding rounds are different, but some elements will seem familiar. As with the series A round, there will be some investors that just won't be interested, however compelling the offer. Either they won't operate in the sector concerned, or the funds simply do not issue the sort of cheque size the start-up is seeking. In addition, VCs tend to specialize in particular rounds, and be more inclined to invest in a specific series A, B or C.

Another familiar aspect to subsequent funding rounds is that not all investors take meetings because they have an interest in a particular start-up. As per the first round, some investors will arrange a meeting because they are weighing up whether to invest in a rival firm. They want to use your metrics to shape their decision and your start-up will have the most up-to-date accurate figures in the sector. I have had this experience with a few VCs in particular who I have spoken with more times than I care to imagine. They arrive insisting that they are super-keen to invest in Starling *this time*. But, each time, they go off and invest in our rivals. (It is always satisfying when they finally admit that they made the wrong decision!) It's frustrating, but there is not much that can be done to stop it.

Female founders will also experience an extended level of scrutiny from some all-male investment teams. Despite the fact that the female-led start-up has proved itself, and has evidence to that effect, there is often a scepticism about their forecasts. It has happened to me throughout my entrepreneur journey, even when Starling became the first of the new breed of challenger banks to go into profit, reporting an operating profit of £0.8 million in October 2020. Even though I had the most well thought-out and justified business plans, these plans were not always believed. It's not just investors, either. In my annual results letter of 2022 I forecast a more than 30 per cent return on tangible equity, which was reported widely with huge scepticism. A year later when I announced we had, indeed, achieved the predicted metric, one journalist had the good grace to note that Starling Bank had indeed delivered yet again. This is not the only time that my well-researched forecasts have been ridiculed and this was especially the case when we publicly committed to a 7 per cent market share of business banking, which was seen as impossible by commentators. Why am I noting this here? To show that the prejudice won't just go away as you progress through funding rounds, even once you meet all your forecasts and show tangible evidence of success in growing a business. It won't happen all the time, but it will continue.

How, then, do subsequent rounds differ? For a start, a lot more people will be involved. During the initial rounds, it is a negotiation between the incoming investors led by the lead, and the founders. In subsequent rounds it is much more complicated, with the incoming investors negotiating with both the founders and the investors from previous rounds. If each of the investors and the founders have legal teams then it is likely that the costs will escalate. The incoming investors, especially at higher valuations and round sizes, may want to have a specialist firm support their due diligence process, which is the process the investors follow to check that claims made by founders in their pitches are actually backed up by data, software or customer numbers. Whilst in the early stages there is not much due diligence, the more mature the company, then the more complex task this is. At this point the founding team need to be very organized and structured in populating the virtual data room (VDR) and answering the hundreds of questions that investors will pose.

Start-ups will have a lot more numbers under their belt by this stage and evidence about what is working and what isn't. Founders should be wary of 'jazz hands', saying everything is wonderful. Yes, they want to tell a positive story. However, they need to show they are aware of challenges because every business has challenges. What is important to investors is that the founders and the team have a plan to solve them.

Sophie Adelman, Co-Founder, Multiverse and One Garden

Founders should expect to be under even more personal scrutiny by partners, along with their senior team. They have been running the start-up for a while now, and deployed the money they received from the previous round. New investors need to be confident of their track record to date and that everyone is capable of getting to the next stage of growth. If there are any doubts about how well the growth strategy has been handled, investors may ask for extra oversight and control as one of their terms.

There are, at least, some ways in which the second round will seem easier. Series A investors may open their contacts books and introduce the founder to other VCs they know. They may also have some useful insights and advice to smooth the way. Even if the start-up is generating introductions itself, there should be more interest elsewhere, among VCs that were previously not interested in even taking a meeting. The fact that a start-up has raised before gives it credibility. It's even better if the first raise was from a VC that everyone knows, or that has a reputation for picking winners. Depressingly, the opposite works too, and this can penalize female founders who have taken investment from less established funds, which are often the only resource which will back them.

Perhaps one of the largest points of difference is around the presentation and pitch deck. During the first round, a start-up doesn't have any metrics.

A prototype may not have been built yet, so the founder is discussing a concept. While they are convinced this is what the market has been waiting for all along, no one knows this for certain. By this time, though, the product will have gone live. Real customers will be buying a real product. There will be numbers showing how it is performing.

VCs are not simply interested in revenue and costs. These are important metrics, but are not the sole indicators of a company's potential growth. Investors know that keeping track of what makes a business successful is what will help it scale rapidly. These metrics will do the heavy lifting when it comes to selling the round. As before, founders need to get to grips with the lingo and this means understanding the main metrics that will excite prospective investors. There are hundreds of them, but some key ones to know include:

- **Customer acquisition cost (CAC)**
  Customers generate revenue, but getting them to buy and trust a product comes at a cost. CAC verifies how much is being spent to attract each customer. It's calculated by choosing a specific time period, such as a quarter, and dividing the cost of marketing and sales by the number of customers gained during that period. Investors expect CAC to be high early on, as a start-up tries to build its customer base. However, a rising CAC will set off alarm bells that the business may be floundering.

- **Retention rate**
  It may cost five times more to acquire a new customer than to keep an existing one, so it makes sense to look after them. Oddly, though, start-ups often focus far more of their efforts on building up new customer numbers. Investors will look at the retention rate to make sure that enough effort is being made to nurture existing customers. Retention rates don't, of course, tell the whole story. Investors will know that the number of existing customers can include inactive ones who are buying less of the product. It can also include churn – those customers that have stopped buying it altogether. They expect a start-up to be on top of the numbers of inactive customers and churn.

- **Average revenue per user (ARPU)**
  As the name suggests, this is the amount of top line revenue that one customer contributes over a given time period. This can also be broken down by customer segment or product type if a start-up produces a number of products.

- **Customer lifetime revenue (CLR)**
  This metric is a little more difficult during the early stages of a start-up. As more data emerges, it will be possible to determine how much an individual customer is worth during the time they are with the start-up.

- **Referral rate**
  Word-of-mouth advertising, when a customer recommends a product to family and friends, is the most powerful form of promotion. The higher the referral rate, the lower the CAC.

- **Burn rate**
  Burn rate shows how quickly a start-up is spending its money. Expect investors to give this metric intense scrutiny, because they need to see that cash is not being wasted on unnecessary expenses.

The metrics will vary for each category of business. One of the problems we had at Starling was that we were a new category – a consumer-focused, technology-first start-up bank. VC firms are all organized by sector, whether it is consumer or tech, and tend to look at businesses using their own set of metrics. For a long while, no one seemed able to work out whether our metrics should be in the same category as Facebook or Barclays. We soon found that when we spoke to tech-orientated investors they wanted to talk in tech metrics, while VCs that invested in financial institutions spoke in bank metrics. We had to be quite agile and get to know all the possible metrics. If we hadn't done so, investors wouldn't have understood the metrics we were using and would have asked us questions that we didn't understand.

Getting noticed

It is inevitable that any substantial investment round will get some attention from the press. This is especially so if the founder of the business is a woman. It is still rare enough to constitute a news item, and stories of a funding round sometimes move out of the specialist media and into the mainstream media. The focus of the story will invariably be the woman herself, instead of the fantastic progress her start-up.

The same advice stands as before, in that we should take every advantage we can get and use the opportunity to shine a spotlight on our businesses. This may take some careful manoeuvring around reporters in order to get the right message across. But you've done the hard bit: getting their attention.

Any founder should be especially wary at a time like this. There is an entire industry set up to 'help' start-ups spend the results of investment rounds. Rest assured, they are watching the news like a hawk. Each time Starling raised any cash, I would be inundated with offers to buy a yacht, or private plane, or any number of status symbols I did not have any interest in and could not remotely afford either. It is quite probable that the number of these 'offers' will increase in line with the amount of coverage received. The first thing to say here is: this is a bit of a nonsense. If a founder raises £20 million, they don't instantly get £20 million in their personal bank account. They are not suddenly able to buy a yacht or a supercar. It is not 'their' money to spend on themselves. That doesn't seem to put off the luxury product marketing teams, though. The best advice is: don't let it become a distraction.

Sadly, a large injection of cash can bring out the worst in some people, even those who were trusted allies. One female founder who had achieved a substantial raise for her start-up tells how a group of 20 new faces appeared in the office almost overnight. When she asked her CTO about them, he said that they were working on a freelance basis to speed up progress towards the next phase, now they had the funding. It took a little digging, but she discovered that the 20 coders were all mates of the CTO. A few of them were skilled, but most were not even close to that. It was, to all intents and purposes, a money grab. The founder in question fired all the new faces and the CTO, and she also had the last laugh. She gave notes to all the good coders, asking them to come back to work for her. In the end, she recruited some good people, but the circumstances were far from ideal.

While any raise should be celebrated, it is not the pinnacle of success. It is another stage in the progress towards exit. Rather than getting carried away, it is more important to look at all the promises that were made during the raise, and make a careful timetable of all the metrics that need to be met to fulfil them. If, at any point, there is a danger that things are not going to plan, the investor's expectations will need to be managed.

Careful thought needs to be given to how the money is spent. Some start-ups are cautious about using investment and even put off hiring. This is, of course, a bad idea. If the plan needed these new hires and the funding was secured on the back of the plan, make the hires. Likewise, though, if a large spend was not in the plan, don't suddenly prioritize something that is well over and above what was originally pitched.

As with series A, there will be huge highs and lows in these subsequent funding rounds. There will even be times when things go to the wire, only to be snatched away at the last moment. As Joanna Jensen describes below, there is little else that can be done other than to pick yourself up, dust yourself down and throw yourself back into the fray.

Childs Farm had a listing in Waitrose and was on the brink of getting one with Boots, which would have been a real game-changer. I was looking for £3 million, which was a big chunk of capital for us, but we were too early-stage for the investment criteria the VC fund we were speaking with had. Yet, one of the principals said, 'No, we're going to do it. I really believe in this business.' The negotiations went on for months and cost an awful lot of money, probably about £150,000 on legal fees alone.

Four days before we were due to sign, they pulled out. The principal didn't call to tell me; he got one of his colleagues to do it. I got straight on the train to London to try to get him to reconsider, and was hyperventilating so much that the guard put me in a first-class cabin so I could calm down. I was OK by the time I banged on the door of his office, but the principal didn't want to know. To make things even worse, he arranged a conference call with Boots and told them it was very unlikely we'd be able to make enough product for the listing now, because we'd lost his investment.

I arranged an emergency meeting with Boots and went in there all guns blazing. I was prepared to fight my corner. Their response completely floored me. The category director said, 'Joanna, we love your brand. We think you are on to something. What do you need from us?' They offered me support and investment there and then.

I decided not to take their investment because I didn't want to restrict myself to one retailer. But their reaction gave me the confidence boost I needed. I called our manufacturer, who was just boarding a plane to Chicago, and he said straight away he'd bank-roll us. 'You're going into Boots,' he said. 'The rest we'll sort out later.' He lent us a lot of money over the next 12 months and gave us the breathing space we needed. I was so glad we didn't go with that VC now. It would have been a nightmare and the biggest mistake we ever made. These things all happen for a reason.

Joanna Jensen, Founder, Childs Farm

CHAPTER FOURTEEN

Leading a unicorn

Founding a business and then successfully scaling it to become a major player in the market is rare, but it does happen. To achieve this remarkable feat of scaling, a business needs to perfect the seemingly elusive combination of a great product, perfect timing, a determined founder, a talented and hardworking team, some chutzpah and a little bit of luck. Anyone who has succeeded in combining these elements deserves hearty congratulations. But, as I know from experience, they're very unlikely to kick back to celebrate. Founders of successful high-growth businesses never like to get too comfortable. Sure, they acknowledge the wins, but then quickly move on to 'What next?' There needs to be a constant sense of momentum, or things will grind to a halt.

It has been said that leading a high-growth business is like hanging onto a rocket ship. It's tense, exhausting and all consuming. Founders will think of nothing else. I stepped down as CEO of Starling Bank in May 2023, and yet it is still my first thought every day. For the first few weeks, I had to make a conscious effort to not pick up the phone to a colleague every time I had an idea. I stepped aside because the business had reached a size where it was felt that separating my two roles as a leader of the business and a large shareholder was in its best interests. The roles of shareholder and chief executive do differ. I do, however, remain on the board as a non-executive.

What, then, can I share about the experience of running a high-growth business? My first observation is that the realization you are running a venture of significant size can hit you quite suddenly. For months and years, every waking hour is devoted to getting people to notice you and the start-up. The number of hours spent in meetings, knocking on doors, or appearing on Zooms will be into the thousands. Every ounce of energy will have been put into selling the idea of the start-up to everyone, whether key hires, investors or customers. You'll find yourself doing all sorts of things you maybe never dreamed of before. Perhaps the most memorable for me was spending a cold, damp Sunday wandering up and down the muddy try-lines of Marlow rugby club giving away Starling-branded gloves to the parents watching their kids play rugby. Then, one day, you'll realize people *have* noticed you. Not only that, but they are also talking about your company. Satisfied customers will speak to friends and family urging them to try your product, and sales will soar exponentially. In our case, I realized that our distinctive teal-coloured Starling cards were being used everywhere I looked. When I pop into a coffee shop and see people using our cards and I still get excited about it (although I also want to interrupt their conversation to ask why they don't use their phones to pay for their cappuccino). This is what entrepreneurs *dream* about in the early days.

There's a downside, too. As already noted, female founders always come under intense scrutiny, and successful female founders will experience this to the extreme. Every action will be picked over by the media. If someone senior leaves, there will be question marks over whether female bosses are too harsh, or not harsh enough. (I call this boiled egg syndrome. Female leaders are always criticized for being too forthright, or not forthright enough. Never perfect.) News about profits, or otherwise, will be picked over in minute detail.

Something else will happen, too, again because of the rarity value: female founders will find themselves being approached by senior political figures, established business leaders and trade bodies, and invited to all sorts of events. It's perceived to be good to have a successful woman around because it implies that the group doing the inviting are doing their bit for diversity. Of course, if not careful, it's easy to end up being permanently showcased, rushing from one event to another. But, you can't allow yourself to become distracted. Running a high-growth business is a 24/7 job.

Switching out of start-up mode

> The secret to scaling is actually quite simple. Any business can scale. You either find a new market to go to, or a new region, or you find a new product to sell to the same customer. Anything can get bigger by just expanding your mindset and thinking: can this be global?
>
> **Sam Smith, Founder, finnCap**

Having been there from the start, it is hard to switch from being the person who does everything, into the person who *leads* a team that does everything. Some founders struggle with this changing role, believing that they can still get stuck in wherever needed. Their role is, however, substantially different from the days of leading a plucky start-up. Things can't stay the same. If you think they can, you are deluding yourself.

The role now is to release the talent of the team, letting them know that they are respected and that their judgement is sound. Leaders set the context and let the team tell them how to move things forward to realize the goals set out in the carefully honed investor pitches. I always liken this balance to finding the drumbeat of the business. Think about any large corporate. They'll have a routine in place that has been there forever. The sales figures will come in on a Monday, and there will be a sales meeting every Tuesday afternoon and so on. Everyone on the team can rely on that happening. It is the drumbeat that keeps the organization powering forward. Founders need to create that drumbeat in their own organization. They set the pace that everyone follows. I mentioned earlier the Starling ritual of a demo every Friday, accompanied by bacon sarnies and a seemingly never-ending expanded menu. These demos were a drumbeat, driving the momentum to keep developing and improving our app. There would be a drumbeat for all other aspects of the business, too, from regulatory submissions, to product development, to investor updates. Each one is driven by the person at the top. The CEO is the pacemaker.

None of this is to say that founders should forget everything they have learned to date. There are some elements to start-up life that should very much carry on. Something I was always very keen to protect was the *immediacy* of a start-up. I know from my corporate career how decision-making grinds to a halt in big businesses, as one person awaits the nod from various stakeholders throughout the organization. There's a long, tortuous process of back-and-forth while teams tweak documents, re-present them and then go away to change them again. At Starling, we kept to the system where any new strategy begins with a 'press release' and relevant team members are invited to view the Google document and give their input. Then, we'd sit in a room and have a debate about it. That way, we get instant feedback on the quality of the idea, and we can move on quickly from there.

Earlier, I mentioned the £100 million grant to deliver the UK's best bank for SMEs. To secure it, we had to agree to a long list of undertakings to meet the terms. Two years in, though, with our business accounts launched and already building a significant market share, we wanted to make some changes to what we were going to deliver. These changes were going to improve the offer, but we still needed approval from the fund's administrators. Once we made our submission, the administrators returned with a bunch of questions that they wanted answered within a very short timeline. It was like being propelled back into the early days. The Starling team got a Google document up on a laptop screen, with the administrator's questions listed down one side and spaces for our answers on the other. Everyone involved, including me, piled into the room and worked together, checking and debating facts and contributing to the document. We didn't have time for someone to work on the document alone, write the answers, then send it up and down the chain of command for approval at various levels. It was just much better to work like a start-up and get the job done there and then. It was intense, with a bunch of Starling people dipping in and out, but it was hugely satisfying too.

Likewise, we retained the same attitude to moving fast and innovating. As a business scales, it would be easy to get hamstrung about making mistakes and the potential size of the backlash. Founders can't allow this to happen. They need to keep pushing and innovating. If we make a mistake, we always say so. We're open about it too, saying, 'We've taken the wrong direction, but we can easily backtrack.' And we can. Our teams use Slack to communicate with one another on projects, so it is very easy to see when, where and how a project went off course and to learn from it. There is no sense of assigning blame. The focus is on getting it right. We are very precise and self-reflective about what we do and everyone is proud of that.

Growth won't be linear, either, and this is where thinking like a start-up comes into its own. Occasionally, as Joanna Jensen found, sales will become stratospheric overnight, and a business needs to be prepared to move at lightning speed.

When it comes to high growth, you need to be careful what you wish for. A parent of a child with eczema put a post on Facebook. It showed a before-and-after picture of her daughter's hands having used our baby moisturiser, and they went from sore and bloody to looking like new. She'd tagged us in her post and wrote; 'We tried this for two weeks and look at the difference. I can't recommend it enough.' Suddenly our sales went through the roof. Before we'd even realized what was happening, the post had been shared 20,000 times.

I spoke to our PR agency and said, 'How can we make the most of this?' We spoke to the mum who did the original post and she agreed to be interviewed by the *Daily Mail*, and their article was then syndicated across the UK press and internationally. By June, the original post had been shared 45,000 times. I was on holiday in Cornwall when I got a call from my head of sales to say that online sales had gone mad, selling £1,000 of stock every five minutes. It was clear we wouldn't have enough stock to meet all the orders that were flooding in. Even if they stopped right then, it would take seven weeks to fulfil them. We decided to take the Hermès Handbag approach to our lack of stock and trade on the scarcity of the baby moisturiser. We put a note on the website telling consumers that the stock was flying out of the door, and in order to secure some they should sign up to our waiting list. We also got back to everyone who had already made an order and asked them to please bear with us on dispatch, and they were incredibly understanding. Then, the retailers started calling asking for more stock...

The whole Childs Farm team rallied together, and our suppliers worked around the clock, but it wasn't until the following February that we caught up with stock levels, nearly one year after that post went viral. During that time, we pulled all our marketing spend. There was no point as we couldn't make enough stock to fulfil orders as it was.

Then, one year later, it happened all over again. The next viral post was shared 65,000 times and we sold £1.5 millions of baby moisturiser in a week. The CEO of Morrison's called in person and said, 'Please make sure we get our quota.' Asda gave us gondola ends by the checkout to ensure the baby moisturiser was visible to shoppers, and the sell-through was nuts. Luckily, we had better stock levels and, vitally, we had experience in dealing with a sell-out. This meant that we could deliver on retailer forecasts as well as meet around 50 per cent of their additional demand. Everyone did well, and we quickly became the number one brand in the category in the UK.

It was the most exhausting thing that had ever happened to me, in a fabulously positive way. We were begging and borrowing and doing whatever we could to get these products made. Would I have done anything different?

No. You can't tie up your cash in stock in the hope that a phenomenon like this happens. It is rare. And the experience taught us so much. For example, if the product is outstanding, people will wait for it. Plus, of course, it showed the importance of having good relationships with all your supply chain so they will willingly work to fulfil your orders at pace and share in the excitement of your success.

Joanna Jensen, Founder, Childs Farm

Leading effectively

One strong parallel between leading a start-up and a high-growth business is that it is a 24/7 affair. There will always be something to do. However, once a business has scaled, or is in the process of scaling, it is crucial that founders do the *right* things. The secret to getting this right is to be very structured about your time.

While a full-time CEO, I could still react at a moment's notice when something needed my attention but, for the most part, my weeks were very structured. Sundays were my strategy day, where I'd mull over all the issues we were dealing with at the time and I'd finish the day by writing an email about the big, strategic things we needed to do. I'd also share a list of what still had to be attended to, but where I hadn't yet quite figured out what to do. Weekdays were very much about interacting with various members of the team for successive short periods and were quite operational. Twice a week, I'd get together with the executive team to go through strategy. My goal was to get into the detail of everything, and if I couldn't find an answer, I would keep questioning until I did. To keep to this schedule often meant being ruthless about my time.

A big part of a founder's responsibilities is to maintain a careful eye on the finances. It may be tempting to take big financial leaps now there is more revenue coming in, or even to relax a little, but taking an eye of the ball financially has destroyed many businesses. Good financial planning is crucial now. Managing costs effectively to aim for a long-term growth curve can only be achieved by controlling project costs, spending less money than you make while still maintaining top levels of service, quality and innovation, and balancing headcount with revenue.

> Everyone expects entrepreneurs to be all about ideas and creative projects, but they need to behave like CEOs too. That means attending to the hygiene of the business. We can't keep looking forward. High-growth businesses require constant maintenance.
>
> Entrepreneurs see things other people don't see. I don't work on computers, which is bizarre to say, since I run an online company. Instead, I use physical spreadsheets showing all my data so I can *see* what's going on. As long as I've got the figures showing what's happening in my business, I can see where there are problems. I can spot things even my CFO can't spot. It's very easy to get swept along by the momentum and numbers that get bigger and bigger. But if you ignore the business hygiene, it can get very bloated.
>
> **Christy Foster, Founder, Online4Baby**

Aside from the finances, one of the most challenging aspects to running a high-growth business is leading a sizeable team. When it comes to head-count, Starling's rate of growth has been astonishing. We have always been a lean team, but we've grown exponentially from 62 employees in 2016, through to 1,750 in 2022, to 3,000 just one year on. Founders of high-growth businesses will all experience that moment where they no longer know everyone who works for them. One day, you will walk into an office and barely recognize a single face. This has implications for so many aspects of leadership.

Take the idea of culture, which as everyone know is a big buzzword in start-ups and, in particular, among tech-based disruptors. For a long time, I had always been very reluctant to produce the ubiquitous 'culture deck' which lays out 'how we do things around here'. My focus was simply that everyone understood that the customer experience came first and our technology was the way forward. I didn't want to go down the route of rules for everything. One of the few rules we had was a ban on creating PowerPoint presentations for each other internally. As everyone knows, they are just a great way to waste time, or avoid doing the real work of looking after our customers. Everyone should be focused on actually producing things, rather than having meetings or finding a way to delegate their work.

As the number of Starlings grew, I realized that newcomers to the team wouldn't just pick up the culture. Besides, many of the team worked at our offices in Southampton, Dublin, Cardiff and Manchester, or remotely, and even more so following the pandemic. It was time to document our core values. As is my way, I spent a long time poring over business books to find the best ideas, and then I put them to the team. We managed to distil the Starling brand into five values: listen, own it, keep it simple, do the right thing and aim for greatness.

The thinking behind the final list was that we always wanted to listen to customers in order to deliver the features they wanted. Own it was a succinct way of describing our process of dealing with things that went wrong – we never wanted anyone at Starling Bank to hide from bad decisions as there is always something that can be learned from them. Keep it simple was exactly what I was trying to do from the very start. I didn't want all the committees, paperwork and consultants to govern how we ran the bank. Working for customers means making the right decisions, quickly. Aiming for greatness and doing the right thing described what we had driven towards from the very beginning. We were always trying to punch above our weight but everything we did was always evaluated against our brand. Now everyone who joins Starling understands our culture.

Something all founders also need to accept is that some of the early team will move on. Not everyone will be there for the whole journey. While some were perfect for the start-up phase, they may not have the skills or experience to shine in a large business. The skill requirements of the job change, and the composition of the team will need to reflect that. In my own case, the opposite was true. With hindsight, I can say I was less equipped to live through the twists and turns of scaling a scrappy start-up, but fortunately I somehow muddled through. When we reached a certain size, though, I felt more comfortable. And this is a point all high-growth founders will also need to get to grips with: are they the right person to lead the business once it reaches a certain size? Not all founders simply morph into being perfect CEOs of a large corporate. A completely different set of leadership skills is required. There is no shame in bringing in an experienced pair of hands to lead a business through its next stage of growth. Many start-up founders do this, taking a sidestep into a less hands-on role.

Staying resilient

I came across eBay shortly after it started. At the time, we were working 60 different markets, from Manchester to Leeds. I thought, I am driving miles and miles each day and eBay means I can sit at home and sell without that much effort. The first night in, I sold 16 expensive prams. When I took them to the Post Office the next day, it completely blocked up their storage space, so I needed to get a parcel contract. We got bigger and bigger after that.

I was at an event and a German banker who was funding a big company on eBay leaned across the table and said, 'Christy, we are going to shut you down within twelve weeks.' We were doing £1 million a year with eBay by that time, which was a lot in those days. About twelve months later, the same banker called and asked me to buy all their stock because they'd had to shut the company down. We'd outtraded them.

A lot of people do a lot of nasty things to get where they need to get to. I'm always very professional. What I always think is, I'll hurt you in the pocket down the line. And that's what I love. I love the chase. I love beating people – but in a professional way. I thrive on the challenge.

Christy Foster, Founder, Online4Baby

No one will ever be as fully committed to a business as its founder or co-founders. All being well, the rest of the team will be proud of working for the start-up, but they won't see the jeopardy it gets into on the roller-coaster ride towards success. They won't know that if a particular set of numbers isn't reached that month, or that next round of funding secured, the business may need to close. They won't experience the fear of being responsible for a group of people and their dependents. That's stressful. And, of course, that stress doesn't just disappear once the business reaches a certain size.

I have asked myself; if I knew what it was going to be like when I started in 2014, would I still have done it? If anyone had told me that I would have more than 500 meetings with investors, would I have still decided this was a good idea? I am a rational person and on paper this does not seem like a sensible way to live one's life. I think the naivety about what lay ahead helped. If someone asked me to start another bank today, I'd probably say 'No way.' Not knowing what lay ahead helped.

I prefer to look at it in another, more positive way, which is, I realize, how I deal with pressure. Did those hundreds of meetings actually help me build a better business? I think they probably did. It was like having a really, really tough business coach. Plus, if I didn't have to work so hard to raise money, I might have spent it more easily, without thinking about every pound that went out. I still believe that a great deal of the reason why Starling has been so successful is because we had to fight really hard to build it.

The other character trait that has always spurred me on is the deep-seated desire to prove everyone else wrong. I used my frustration about being discounted, knocked back and disparaged so often, and turned it around, vowing to prove everyone wrong. It's a powerful motivator and many other successful female founders do the same thing.

The resilience of a founder will have an impact on the success – or otherwise – of their start-up. Whatever reserves of strength you have, or whatever keeps you keeping on, is what you will need to draw upon when things are at their most difficult.

I grew up in Bradford, one of the poorest cities in England, and was the first person in my family to go to university. When I got there, they laughed at me because of my accent and the way I used to dress. It was the 1990s and I had blond streaks in my hair and wore big gold hoops in my ears. I was clearly not the typical university type amongst all these publicly educated schoolkids. Do you know what? It fed my fire. I became on a mission to prove everybody wrong and that I could do it. People underestimated me because I'm a woman. I'm just automatically discounted. I take great delight in proving people wrong and achieving things no one expected.

I'm constantly thinking about ways to move forward. A lot of people make New Year's resolutions, and spend a great deal of time reflecting on what they will do better in the coming year. I think we should all commit to a period of reflection like this on a more regular basis, like once every month. It is very easy to get caught up in the whirlwind of life when running a growing business, but taking an hour out to say, OK, what are my priorities, can make all the difference.

Doing something like this might seem 'important' but not 'urgent', but I disagree. I think we need to be ruthless about prioritizing time to think.

Alex Depledge, Founder and CEO, Resi

Something all female founders should realize is that there are not as many of us, but we are a powerful network. Not only that, we fully understand that challenges that we face with all sorts of people trying to put us back in our place. It is so good to have people beside you, people to whom you can say, 'Why is it so difficult?'

When you put yourself out there, you do feel in a vulnerable position. You've exposed yourself to an awful lot of challenge. I've literally cried and cried over some things. I've walked out of the office and screamed into the open air. What works best, though, is picking up the phone to my peers, particularly my female peers who can completely empathize with my position. There are some amazing and hugely supportive WhatsApp groups out there. They are filled with women venting forth, telling stories about things that shouldn't be happening. It's amazing how much of it is going on, all the time. But, here's the thing – sharing it via these groups is all you need. It is like a super-fast counselling session. Getting it out into the open stops it eating you up and messing with your head. It's like a safe space.

   If there was one great thing that could happen, it would be that women could be more confident in sharing the truth on a wider basis. They wouldn't be afraid of a social media or mainstream media pile-on, attacking them for something they've experienced that is just wrong. I've encouraged other female founders to shout about goes on, alongside me. If I shout, you shout, we all shout together. That's how we all get found, and we all get heard.

Zandra Moore, Founder and CEO, Panintelligence

It is also important not to lose sight of the fact that the start-up team has been through a lot to get here, too. Many may have given up good jobs to take part in the journey and it will have been a tough climb for them, too. While it is traditional for stock options to be reserved for the top team, it was important to me that everyone should reap the rewards of what we have done to make Starling a success. In February 2020, Starling announced that all employees had been allocated an equal conditional share award, regardless of seniority.

What next?

A well-known venture capitalist sought me out at an awards dinner towards the end of 2022.

   'What's it like to have won?' he said, with a conspiratorial smile.

   For a few moments, I was lost for words. Won? The awards had not been announced yet that evening. Did he have some inside information? 'What do you mean?' I asked.

'Well for many years you were trailing – you were not cool,' he said. 'Now you are leading the pack.'

We'd had a brilliant year, yes and were in profit, unlike all of our closest rivals in fintech, and were giving the establishment a run for their money in the business and current account market. But won? For some reason, I hated that word. Any hint of punching the air in victory, or recognition that our diligent hard work had paid off, felt just too complacent.

'No, no, we still have so much to do,' I replied. 'Don't dismiss everyone else.'

That is, of course, true. The journey is not over until it is over. Like all high-growth businesses, we have discussed the exit with our investors. There's been speculation about an IPO, or us either being bought out by, or buying, a competitor. Time will tell.

The big question is, if and when there is a successful exit, what next? Do you head off into the sunset and enjoy a well-earned break? Or, do you throw yourself back into it and do it all over again? Speak to almost any founder in the situation and mention the r-word – retirement – and you will most likely be greeted with a look of horror. No matter what age they are at exit, they are still driven and eager to create and build something. We identify ourselves through what we do as entrepreneurs. Take away the entrepreneur part and we don't feel quite right.

The nature of the exit will impact what happens next. If, for example, the business has been sold to a rival firm, then there will be a non-compete clause for a period of time. This will restrict the range of any subsequent start-up. An expert in, say, medtech, will need to specialize in another field entirely. Then, there is the question of money. There is a common misconception that when there is an IPO a founder is then rolling in cash overnight. Some will keep their shares in the business out of choice, and others, depending on the percentage shareholding, will face restrictions on the amount of cash they can get out in the short term.

Having said all that, it is in many ways a lot easier to build a start-up second time around. Any entrepreneur that successfully exits will, all being well, have at least some capital behind them. This means they will be able to get a lot further on with any new business before needing to pitch for outside investment. When you invest your own money you have more control. Plus, when you do go out into the market, you'll know better how the system works. You'll probably be a bit more cynical too and less likely to accept something that is clearly not in your best interests. Most of all, though, you'll understand how it all works. Having gone through it all before, it is less arduous the second time around.

There will be elements to starting again that are not as straightforward. Earlier, we talked about the option to try and fail with elements of the business such as the marketing campaign, because no one is watching. The opposite is true the second time around, and particularly so for female founders, given how unusual they are. If they have made a successful exit, all eyes will be on 'what next'. Will they pull it off again?! (The not-too-subtle subtext: *was it a fluke last time?*) Second-time founders should be prepared that whatever they launch will come under immediate scrutiny and, more than likely, a fair share of criticism. Even so, I would not allow this to temper the approach. In this case, the advice from Y-Combinator's Paul Graham still stands: launch something you are ashamed of. In other words, make something and get it out there. If you believe it is 'finished' or 'perfect', it is too late. Again, it still doesn't matter if some potential customers are not impressed. It's irrelevant. As before, it is the feedback, good and bad, that you need.

Ultimately, the choice is yours about whether or not to throw yourself back into it and do it all again. I suspect most entrepreneurs won't be able to resist the lure of getting stuck into another start-up, for all the reasons they were inspired to do so in the first place. Yes, if they have built and exited a high-growth business, they will have fulfilled many of their goals to prove everyone wrong and created the job for themselves they always wanted. However, now there will be a whole new set of reasons to do it and they'll have the confidence that they've done it once already. Who knows what can be achieved next time? There are few true entrepreneurs that would be able to resist.

Afterword

When setting up Starling Bank, there was a lot I didn't know about seeking investment for, and then leading, a high-growth enterprise, so I had to figure it out as I went along. As I moved through a seemingly endless number of pitches, I frequently mused on why the world is dominated by a handful of serial entrepreneurs who have started, and then exited, one business after another. I concluded that they'd learned the playbook and knew how it was done. The hope is that the tips, stories and advice shared here will go some way to delivering a version of that playbook, one that will inspire and help the next generation of female entrepreneurs to build high-growth businesses.

Should you start with the aim of creating a high-growth business? Entrepreneurs that gain even modest success will do well financially, possibly netting thousands of pounds, if not millions, which is, of course, life changing. But the odds are that the majority of entrepreneurs won't succeed in founding and scaling a high-growth business. In fact, there is probably a less than one in a thousand chance that they will. That doesn't mean you shouldn't try, though, and my wish is that, after reading this book and hearing the amazing stories of these female entrepreneurs, you will be tempted to do so.

There is a huge opportunity here for female entrepreneurs. Positive change is already happening to pave the way for more female-led high-growth businesses, and it is being led from all sides. The VC community is already upping its game and working towards making the investment environment more welcoming to women, at long last embracing the highly investible qualities that make us ideal entrepreneurs. By convening the task-force, the UK government has signalled a political will to create a better environment that will help women-led businesses to scale up and thrive. Meanwhile, many already-successful female founders are going out of their way to help the next generation to find a way over, under and around the challenges they face.

Obstacles do remain, though. Female founders will still find themselves facing discrimination now and again. But another way to look at it is to say that this happens at every stage of a woman's life, whether or not she starts a business. Early on, they're discriminated against in the workplace because one day they might have a baby. Then, if they don't have a baby, they are discriminated against, too. I've heard people asking women whether they should possibly resort to IVF! They'll be judged because they are not married with two children. Then they'll be singled out because they are going to enter menopause.

Men don't have this. No one mentions pre- and post-baldness. When men have a young family, no one wonders (often out loud) if they'll be leaving work early to pick up kids from school. There are different ways female entrepreneurs can approach this ongoing discrimination. We can give it credibility, and campaign to change it. Or we can ignore it. I prefer a combination of the two. I'm outspoken when I need to be and do my utmost to support my fellow female entrepreneurs, but I also believe action can be more powerful than words. My goal is to prove my worth, so it is impossible for others to discriminate. Day-by-day, bit-by-bit I have achieved everything people said I couldn't do. One of my career memories that still makes me smile was receiving an email from a headhunter who told me I hadn't got a job I really wanted because I was not a 'digital native'. The irony is never lost on me, having somehow managed to 'muddle my way through' this hurdle to establish one of modern banking's biggest success stories, which also happens to be an entirely digital offering. The truth is, I did have all the relevant skills I needed after all. It's the interviewer's loss they didn't see that. I know there are many more women like me who have been dismissed and who are dying to prove the naysayers wrong. My advice is to do just that because there really is nothing that is quite so satisfying. I very much look forward to many, many more female founders doing the same.

If there was a formula to scaling a high-growth business and successfully exiting, then it wouldn't be so difficult to succeed. But there isn't. There is, however, a lot of information in this book that will help smooth the journey. To summarize, the main playbook rules for creating a scalable venture are:

- Quickly develop a minimum viable product:
  - Identify a user problem and propose a solution. It can be inspired by personal experience.
  - Discover a large, homogenous potential market.
  - Ensure the total addressable market is large enough.
  - Create a product that is accessible, user-friendly and cost effective.
  - Create a truly unique product – using cutting edge technology.
  - Test the MVP with users to get feedback.

- Hire the right people:
  - Assemble a team by hiring talent who will help drive growth.
  - Team members must have the right skill sets – and share values.
  - Track record and experience are essential.
  - Be decisive about cutting toxic staff or those that are not growing with the business.

- Test the business model:
  - Confirm the product solves real problems, based on user feedback and initial performance.
  - Identify the primary customer and audience.
  - Develop a strong value proposition that sets you apart.
  - Price your product, based on the value it provides, competitor prices and target market.
  - Select sales channels for the product.
  - Run a small-scale rollout to validate the business model.
  - Focus on delivering positive customer experiences.
  - Commit to rapid growth.
  - Be prepared to pivot.

- Understand sources of funding:
  - Bootstrap by building a business using the profits generated by the business, but no external investment.
  - Crowdfund by showcasing product or business idea, communicating the benefits of investment.
  - Obtain loans from banks or other business loan providers.
  - Look into grants and government schemes.
  - Raise VC backed capital through seed and/or series rounds. Prepare pitch deck, pitch, prepare due diligence and negotiate.

- Keys to fundraising success:
  - Have confidence in yourself and your product.
  - Convince yourself that your start-up is worth investing in and then, when you explain it to investors, they will believe you.
  - Demonstrate you know your product inside and out.
  - To appeal to investors, you have to *think* like an investor.
  - Secure the right investment.
  - Timing is everything.
  - There must be a clear path to profit.

- Scale your start-up:
  - Ensure there is market fit.
  - Document and standardize processes for customer acquisition and sales.
  - Expand the business to other locations and markets.
  - Focus on smaller clients when starting out, then shift your focus to bigger clients.
  - Create new departments as needed.
  - Attract new investors.
  - Not all founders can take their business to the next level.
  - Own mistakes and apologise.

- Manage costs effectively:
  - Financial planning and manage cycle to aim for long-term growth curve.
  - Balance headcount with revenue curve.

There are no guarantees in business, still less so when trying to create a unicorn. We are also currently facing a bear market for high-growth enterprises and a downturn in tech stocks. Right now, there is no answer as to how long this downturn will endure, either. However, it is pointless sitting around waiting until the market does recover its full strength. Besides, anecdotal evidence says women shine in crisis situations. When everything is broken, people are more willing to give something new a chance. Tough times ahead for the tech industry could offer the perfect environment for women to buck the trend and make significant progress. We're also great at grasping every opportunity. Put this together with a track record learned from years of pushing back against the naysayers, together with our superpowers such as agility, creativity and determination, and we are an unstoppable force. Women do make the best entrepreneurs; now we need to go out and prove it.

Glossary of start-up and VC lingo

Acqui-hire: One company buys another to acquire the team rather than the products it sells.

Alpha test: The first stage of product testing by the internal team.

Angel investors: High net worth individual who provides funding for early-stage start-ups.

Beta test: The final stage of product testing by users before the item goes out into the market.

Bootstrapping: Building a start-up without external investment but using the profits generated by the business.

Burn rate: The rate at which a start-up consumes cash per month.

Business model: Describes the products and the costs/resources required to create them, to show investors how the start-up will make a profit.

Business plan: The roadmap for a start-up, outlining the objectives and how they will be achieved, covering everything from finances, to marketing, to the team structure.

Buy out: One company buying a controlling share in another.

Cap table: A spreadsheet listing a start-up's stock and who owns it.

Cash flow negative: The amount of money flowing out of the start-up exceeds what is coming in.

Cash flow positive: There is more money going into the start-up than going out.

Cash position: The quantity of cash reserves in a start-up.

Churn rate: Customers won, then lost.

Common stock: Represents ownership and gives stockholders voting rights in proportion to the number of shares owned. Founders may have common stock whilst investors have preference stock.

Competitive advantage: Factors that enable a start-up to outperform others such as price, branding, product quality, distribution and customer service.

Crowdfunding: On a platform, raising money for a start-up from a large group of individuals.

Customer acquisition cost: The total cost of acquiring a new customer.

Debt financing: Raising funding through a loan.

Dilution: A reduction in percentage ownership as new shares are issued.

Disruption: Where a product or service takes over, or changes, an industry or market.

Dividends: Regular payments to shareholders from profits or reserves.

Due diligence: An audit of a start-up's financial and IP records prior to investment.

Equity: Percentage ownership of a start-up.

Equity financing: Raising capital through selling shares to angels, VCs or crowdfunds.

Exit strategy: The plan to cash out an investment, most likely through acquisition, IPO or a management buyout.

Forecast: Projections of performance for a specific period in the future.

Initial public offering (IPO): A company raises investment by selling shares to the public.

Key performance indicator (KPI): A measure of progress towards a target, such as customer conversions or active users.

Lead investor: Organizes and invests in a funding round.

Liquidation preferences: A contract clause that gives investors priority with the proceeds of a liquidation.

Market penetration: Volume of product sold relative to the total estimated target market.

Merger and acquisition: One company buys another.

Minimum viable product (MVP): A very basic version of the product, used to test market interest.

Pitch deck: Presentation to showcase a start-up to potential investors.

Pivot: Where a start-up changes course completely, based on market feedback.

Preferred stock: Special privileges for investors, who may not have voting rights, but minimizes risk if value of investment falls. (See: Common stock)

Pro rata rights: Rights given to an investor to maintain their percentage level of ownership.

Product–market fit: A product that excites customers so much, they will spread the word about it.

Profit margin: A measure of profitability relative to business costs.

Proof of concept: Testing the feasibility of a business idea.

Recapitalization: Restructuring debt and equity to stabilize a start-up's capital structure.

Run rate: Projected financial performance of a start-up based on current performance.

Runway: How long a start-up can sustain itself before running out of cash.

Scalability: A start-up's capacity to grow and increase revenue.

Securities: Tradable financial instruments with monetary value. May be shares or debt in a listed or publicly listed company.

Software as a service (SaaS): Software licensed to businesses on a subscription basis.

Start-up capital: The money needed to get a new business started, used for equipment, inventory, product development and salaries.

Stock options: A contract giving the right, but not obligation, to buy or sell stock at an agreed price within a specific period.

Target market: The group of consumers who will buy your product or service and the focus of your sales and marketing efforts.

Term sheet: Formal but non-binding document outlining terms for investment.

Unicorn: Start-ups valued at over $1 billion.

Valuation: The current worth of a start-up based on projected revenue, customer demand and appetite in the market.

Venture capital: An investor who provides funding to start-ups in exchange for a stake in the company.

Vesting: The concept of founder or employer stock being awarded over time.

Further information

Accelerators and incubators

UK

AccelerateHER: A network for promoting, and sharing businesses founded or run by Women, providing opportunities for their businesses to receive investment and grow. accelerateher.co.uk (archived at https://perma.cc/7NM9-FL56)

CodeBase: CodeBase runs programmes to educate tech start-ups. thisiscodebase.com (archived at https://perma.cc/LKF7-YHZS)

Collider: With offices in London and Amsterdam, focusing on martech, commerce tech and ad tech start-ups, helping them grow through investment and collaboration. collider.io (archived at https://perma.cc/8FSS-DPZT)

Huckletree: Workspaces designed to aid in creativity and innovation, and to surround founders with other like-minded individuals to collaborate and connect. Huckletree. com (archived at https://perma.cc/2LZK-G2X9)

IDEA London: Created by University College London, in partnership with Capital Enterprise, IDEA has successfully generated over 70 start-ups. idealondon.co.uk (archived at https://perma.cc/56B4-7M2T)

Ignite: A programme that takes blockchain start-ups all the way from idea to launch, providing assistance, networking, and funding. ignite.com (archived at https://perma.cc/DAF2-QDFZ)

Imperial College London Enterprise Lab: ICL works with student innovators and future business leaders to make connections and secure future funding. www.imperial.ac.uk/enterprise/students/enterprise-lab (archived at https://perma.cc/9EPR-FVGB)

L Marks: A group with over 80 programmes across the world, offering advice and solutions from industry focused experts. lmarks.com (archived at https://perma.cc/L23G-Y3XD)

Outlier Ventures: With over 500 investors working with Outlier Ventures, the organization promotes itself as the 'world's leading Open Metaverse start-up accelerator'. outlierventures.io (archived at https://perma.cc/7TS5-ZUVM)

Oxygen Accelerator: A tech-focused accelerator group that runs 13-week intensive programmes. oxygenaccelerator.com (archived at https://perma.cc/T9UF-3U6V)

Tech Nation: The previously UK government-backed organization is now owned by the Founders Forum Group, coaching the next generation of founders, connecting them with industry experts and potential backers. technation.io (archived at https://perma.cc/WJ5K-GUSB)

Techstars London: Boasting 'some of the highest quality mentoring available', Techstars has a variety of accelerator and pre-accelerator programmes. techstars.com (archived at https://perma.cc/5RGD-L8Y3)

Worldwide

Alchemist Accelerator: Offering training, advice and networking opportunities, the Alchemist Accelerator has a good success rate when it comes to accelerating early stage start-ups. alchemistaccelerator.com (archived at https://perma.cc/JF5G-3U6E)

AngelPad: AngelPad is a seed-stage start-up incubator that aims to give start-ups the best chance at securing the most funding possible, setting them up with the top experts in their field. angelpad.com (archived at https://perma.cc/W3JS-C9T3)

Berkeley Skydeck: Skydeck is an accelerator and incubator organization, working closely with the University of California, Berkeley. skydeck.berkeley.edu (archived at https://perma.cc/33FW-ANSH)

Blue Startups: Focused on helping scalable technology companies compete globally. bluestartups.com (archived at https://perma.cc/MN4P-CQMG)

Dreamit Ventures: Focusing on health-tech and secure-tech, Series A start-ups. dreamit.com (archived at https://perma.cc/G63J-74F4)

Forum Ventures: Helps founders build B2B SaaS start-ups from scratch, from design all the way through to funding. forumvc.com (archived at https://perma.cc/PC43-4RS8)

Founder Institute: The Founder Institute has seen $1.75 billion raised by its 6,800 plus alumni from more than 100 companies. fi.co (archived at https://perma.cc/8H44-FBNG)

Founders Factory: Backing founders from ideas to seed rounds and beyond, with capital, access to industry-leading corporates, operational support and a community of founders and innovators. foundersfactory.com (archived at https://perma.cc/8H44-FBNG)

Founders Space: A well-connected network of international founders and an innovative online start-up programme. foundersspace.com (archived at https://perma.cc/A6XB-TMYA)

Idealab: The longest-running technology incubator in the world, creating more than 150 companies and over 45 IPOs. idealab.com (archived at https://perma.cc/8YUW-XW67)

Indie Bio: Boasting a 42 per cent intake of female founders, and over $9 billion raised for start-ups. indiebio.co (archived at https://perma.cc/V93A-8JDZ)

MassChallenge: MassChallenge is a nonprofit with an equity free model to accelerate 'high impact' start-ups. masschallenge.org (archived at https://perma.cc/GH3G-GGCD)

Venture Catalysts: With over 300 start-ups created, Venture Catalysts is India's largest incubator. venturecatalysts.in (archived at https://perma.cc/XF8V-NKEY)

Y Combinator: Y Combinator is one of the best-known accelerators, working with over 4,000 start-ups, running three-month programmes twice a year. ycombinator.com (archived at https://perma.cc/H9EF-DW3S)

Associations

British Association of Women Entrepreneurs (BAWE): BAWE is a source of help, networking and education for up-and-coming female entrepreneurs in Britain. bawe-uk.org (archived at https://perma.cc/85N7-PXYH)

British Business Bank: Offers business guidance, mentoring opportunities and information to female entrepreneurs. www.british-business-bank.co.uk/finance-hub/female-entrepreneurs-support-and-mentoring (archived at https://perma.cc/R9EP-6ZZN)

British Private Equity and Venture Capital Association: For over 40-years, the association has been helping with the development of British companies and over 1,500 companies have received investment through the association. bvca.co.uk (archived at https://perma.cc/4KMU-JU9T)

Enterprise Nation: A community of 120,000 people, connecting members to resources and expertise. www.enterprisenation.com (archived at https://perma.cc/X8CZ-DVXW)

Everywoman: Connecting women, businesses and organizations all over the world, offering access to digital tools, female role models and learning resources. www.everywoman.com (archived at https://perma.cc/Q4JE-F5MB)

Female Entrepreneur Association: A global network designed to help women scale their businesses, across a multitude of industries. femaleentrepreneurassociation.com (archived at https://perma.cc/US96-7WWP)

Female Founders Rise: Aims to be the go-to destination for female founders, offering resources such as coaching and investment readiness. www.femalefoundersrise.com (archived at https://perma.cc/Y3F2-YLT7)

Invest in Women Hub: Offering the tools and framework to break down the barriers that women face when starting, or scaling, a business. iiwhub.com (archived at https://perma.cc/3WF3-8JR5)

Prowess: Online information resource for women in business. www.prowess.org.uk (archived at https://perma.cc/S5HL-C4HX)

ScaleUp Institute: A non-profit with the goal of scaling up businesses in the UK to reach their full potential. The Institute also runs the Female Founders Index. scaleupinstitute.org.uk (archived at https://perma.cc/C5NL-XGJS)

The Entrepreneurs Network: A think-tank bridging the gap between entrepreneurs and policymakers. www.tenentrepreneurs.org (archived at https://perma.cc/A4CA-8FT2)

UK Business Angels Association: With over 70 events annually, the Association provides a community of early-stage investors and various programmes to advance start-ups from seed to Series A. ukbaa.org.uk (archived at https://perma.cc/PUL5-MK9U)

UK Finance: One of the leading voices in the banking and finance industry, UK Finance provides data, advice and a community to assist emerging and developing business in the sector. ukfinance.org.uk (archived at https://perma.cc/L984-D4LT)

We Are Tech Women: Helping women in tech maximize their potential. wearetech-women.com (archived at https://perma.cc/7NTY-E4FU)

Women Entrepreneurs UK: Guidance and information on finance, funding and investment. www.womenentrepreneursuk.com (archived at https://perma.cc/YP2T-RBH4)

Networking

EQL:HER: A global network and event series aiming to rebalance gender in the tech sector, with a stated mission to see more women in founding teams, C-suites, start-up boards and investment committees. https://tmt.knect365.com/eql-her/ (archived at https://perma.cc/P3R8-7RZA)

Frederick Women's Business Network and Fund: Offering membership for both individuals and organizations, the network offers opportunities to meet and network with fellow businesswomen. wbnfrederick.org (archived at https://perma.cc/H8JB-7DLN)

Shoosmiths SpHERe network: Networking that aims to bridge the disparities in opportunities offered to male and female entrepreneurs. www.shoosmiths.com (archived at https://perma.cc/8AD3-JWYB)

The Athena Network: The Athena Network is one of the leading networking groups in the UK, holding events across the country. theathenanetwork.com (archived at https://perma.cc/U7LE-2BHZ)

The Better Business Network: Bills itself as offering a fantastic way for founders to network both their business and themselves. thebetterbusiness.network (archived at https://perma.cc/47HD-7WNJ)

The Business Network: The Business Network is runs lunchtime sessions to meet and network with others in a similar line of business. business-network.co.uk (archived at https://perma.cc/NB5Q-KKK2)

The Business Woman's Network: The Business Woman's Network is a virtual networking and online mastermind group. thebusinesswomansnetwork.co.uk (archived at https://perma.cc/U5QL-HUFC)

Up Group: Tech executive search, networking and advisory firm, which runs female-only events. www.theupgroup.com (archived at https://perma.cc/JT8H-B9PP)

Women in Business Network: A organization to support women in business, aiming to build meaningful personal and professional relationships. https://wibn.co.uk (archived at https://perma.cc/3X48-VJC6)

Venture capital supportive to female founders

Ada: Investing in the most important issues the world faces, and the businesses that aim to tackle them. adaventures.com (archived at https://perma.cc/D6HM-76ZB)

Blossom: Founded to 'audaciously challenge how European venture works', prioritizing collaboration and connection. blossomcap.com (archived at https://perma.cc/SGB6-CEQ9)

Diversity VC: Connecting VCs and entrepreneurs to create an industry free from bias. diversity.vc (archived at https://perma.cc/P9VU-3ZEK)

Kindred: Focused on early-stage investment. kindredcapital.vc (archived at https://perma.cc/MV4L-7KUT)

Octopus Investments: Since 2016, 23 per cent of the businesses backed by Octopus investments have a female founder. octopusinvestments.com (archived at https://perma.cc/DWA7-KUD2)

Redrice: The London-based VCs invest at early seed up to Series A, with a focus on B2C consumer brands and technology. redriceventures.com (archived at https://perma.cc/6BPS-PSKP)

Samos Investments: Investments across a range of sectors including consumer internet, digital media, e-commerce, retail and fintech. samos.vc (archived at https://perma.cc/VUR3-62TM)

Speedinvest: Supporting female founders with value-adding events tailored to the needs of female entrepreneurs, as well as investment. www.speedinvest.com (archived at https://perma.cc/8R3N-SDPX)

Suggested reading

As mentioned throughout this book, I am an avid reader and always turn to the printed page when I want to know more about a subject. I've put together a list of some of, what I believe, are the most helpful books for anyone considering, or already running, a start-up. There is just one caveat: in putting together this list, I realize that most of the books originate from the US start-up scene which means that the corporate structures and legal matters may not reflect UK practice. Do check with your lawyer or advisors for up-to-date regulations.

William Draper III (2011) *The Start-up Game: Inside the partnership between venture capitalists and entrepreneurs*

Brad Feld and Jason Mendelson (2011) *Venture Deals: Be smarter than your lawyer and venture capitalist*

Institute of Directors and Pinsent Masons (2007) *Director's Handbook: Your duties responsibilities and liabilities*

Randall Stross (2012) *The Launch Pad: Inside Y Combinator, Silicon Valley's most exclusive school for start-ups*

Noam Wasserman (2012) *The Founder's Dilemmas: Anticipating and avoiding the pitfalls that can sink a start-up*

Product development and pricing

George Berkowski (2014) *How to Build a Billion Dollar App*

Jake Knapp (2015) *Sprint: How to solve big problems and test new ideas in just five days*

Blake Masters and Peter Thiel (2014) *Zero to One Notes on Start Ups, or How to build the future*

Omar Mohout (2015) *Lean Pricing: Pricing strategies for startups*

Eric Ries (2011) *The Lean Startup: How constant innovation creates radically successful businesses*

Scaling

Scott Belsky (2018) *The Messy Middle: Finding your way through the hardest and most crucial part of any bold venture*

Elad Gill (2018) *High Growth Handbook*

Reed Hastings and Erin Myer (2020) *No Rule Rules: Netflix and the culture of reinvention*

Reid Hoffman and Chris Yeh (2018) *Blitzscaling: The lightning-fast path to building massively valuable companies*

Biographies and stories about start-ups

Anne Boden (2020) *Banking on IT*

Ben Horowitz (2014) *The Hard Thing about Hard Things: Building a business when there are no easy answers*

Phil Knight (2016) *Shoe Dog: A memoir by the creator of Nike*

Jessica Livingston (2001) *Founders at Work: Stories of startups' early days*

Some analysis

Ali Tamaseb (2021) *Super Founders: What data reveals about billion-dollar start-ups*

Index

Looking for another book?

Explore our award-winning
books from global business
experts in General Business

Scan the code to browse

www.koganpage.com/general-
business

Printed in the USA
CPSIA information can be obtained
at www.ICGtesting.com
JSHW061911160524
63297JS00011B/218

9 781398 616158